# Captain Blossom in Civvy Street

## ABOUT THE BOOK

Captain Blossom, the picturesque anti-hero of our day, staggers through a series of hilarious misadventures and encounters amongst the remaining Nobs and Snobs of a bomb-ravaged post-War London.

Having successfully avoided sacrificing life or limb for his country, he rejoins some of his pre-War literary friends and mingles in the new post-War boozey demi-monde. Nelson has the post-Waugh touch of being observant while scathing, witty and libidinous, pleasure-seeking and touchingly remorseful, with the effect of an English Woody Allen, while always observing the gentleman's code.

Beneath the hilarity and frivolity, there is a portrait of a generation who emerged by the skin of their teeth from the struggle to save civilization, to discover that they had lost, and that civilization and all that was worth preserving appeared to have gone up in smoke.

## ABOUT THE AUTHOR

Michael Nelson is married, lives in the country, and works alternately as a novelist, television interviewer and journalist. He has written the novels *Knock or Ring, A Room in Chelsea Square, When the Bed Broke* and more recently *Nobs and Snobs*, a study of the vestiges of the English gentleman today.

BY THE SAME AUTHOR

*Knock or Ring*
*A Room in Chelsea Square*
*When the Bed Broke*
*Captain Blossom*
*Captain Blossom Soldiers On*
*Nobs and Snobs*
*Blanket (by Henry Stratton)*

# Captain Blossom in Civvy Street

*Michael Nelson*

Gordon & Cremonesi

© Michael Nelson, 1978

All rights reserved. No part of this publication may be reproduced, stored in a retrieval system, or transmitted in any form or by any means, electronic, mechanical, photocopying, recording or otherwise, without permission in writing from the publishers.

Designed by Heather Gordon
Set in 11 on 13 pt Bembo by Input Typesetting, London
and printed in Great Britain by
The Garden City Press Limited
Letchworth, Hertfordshire SG6 1JS

British Library Cataloguing in Publication Data

Nelson, Michael, b. 1921
   Captain Blossom in civvy street
   1. Title
   823'.9'1F    PR6064.E/    77–30505

ISBN 0-86033-052-4

Gordon & Cremonesi Publishers
London and New York
New River House
34 Seymour Road
London N8 0BE

*Contents*

| | |
|---|---|
| Chapter 1 | 7 |
| Chapter 2 | 35 |
| Chapter 3 | 50 |
| Chapter 4 | 69 |
| Chapter 5 | 82 |
| Chapter 6 | 99 |
| Chapter 7 | 121 |
| Chapter 8 | 138 |
| Chapter 9 | 164 |
| Epilogue | 182 |

# 1

I am sure the Neapolitan Mafia had put out a contract on me. I had well and truly double-crossed them. I had taken their money in considerable quantities and spent it on drink and girls. But when the time had come for me to fulfil my side of the bargain, I had behaved dishonourably.

I had refused to arrange for a consignment of drugs to be driven out of the docks of Naples in my staff car—which was unlikely to be searched by the Military Police. But it was the possibility of discovery, however remote, that had made me go back on my word to the Mafia. I was within a few weeks of being sent back to England to be demobilized after five and a half years of undetected crime and service to His Majesty, King George VI. So it was not surprising that I had been considerably distressed to find myself on the one hand under sentence of death by the Mafia, and on the other faced with the prospect of a Court Martial and a long spell in the glasshouse.

So I can hardly be blamed if I sat in that Dakota aircraft after its take-off from Rome in the August of 1947 with a look of intense relief on my face. For I had been saved by the gun. No doubt that is an unfortunate metaphor in the circumstances. Out of the blue an order had arrived commanding me to report to Rome airport, to fly to the United Kingdom where I would be demobilized.

It is difficult after more than thirty years to remember all that I felt on that day. But I do recollect that I was still upset that the army should have the idiocy to retain my services for more than a year after not only the war in Europe had been won without any help from me, but the war in the Far East as well. However, let bygones be bygones, I told myself. This is the day . . . your personal D-day. You are flying back to your beloved Britain, for which you have fought and died all these years, to your grateful country which will receive you with open arms. You are returning to your family and your loved ones. In a year or two the nightmares of the last five and a half years will have faded; your constant acts of cowardice, your perpetual state of drunkenness will have been forgotten. They will have entered that sweet world of oblivion which you have entered nightly with the aid of the bottle. Not always the best stuff, to be sure. It had not always been whisky, wine and roses. There had been some near scrapes with wood alcohol masquerading under the umbrella of proprietary brands. Never mind. You are still alive. You may have grown fat and your complexion may be blotched with grog blossoms. But you have come through. You have survived.

We had been in the air for scarcely an hour, when I began to feel both hungry and thirsty. I am proud to say that even in my haste to escape the Mafia, I had not forgotten to pack a hamper. I had remembered, even in the sweat of my fear, that only a fool is ever uncomfortable. Luckily the Dakota was not full and, the seat next to me being empty, I proceeded to use it as my side table, and piled it high with salami, pâtés, and two bottles of the best Frascati. The latter was not sufficiently chilled, but under the circumstances it would have to do, as I reckoned that a clapped-out Dakota was unlikely to carry any form of refrigeration.

Before commencing on my first meal of the day I took a quick look round the plane to see if there was anybody I should invite to my table. I did not like what I saw. The aircraft was carrying only Officers, all of whom were of superior rank to me, all of them Lieutenant-Colonels and above. I noticed that as the garlicky smell of the salami wafted along the corridor, some of them looked at me as if I had crawled out from under a stone. I must admit that my battle dress—in fact, my general turn-out—was hardly up to Guards' standard. My shoes were covered with dust, my trousers were without creases, and my campaign medals were the worse for red wine. The Africa Star was almost unrecognizable and could have been mistaken for a Military Cross; the Italian Star, known as the Gelati Gong and one I had always considered vulgar, had something in common with the Distinguished Service Order. I had commanded a German Transport Company prior to my hasty exit from Naples, and my state of disarray was in no way the fault of my German batman, who had turned me out impeccably. I had decided, before leaving, to abandon my khaki drill and return to the

United Kingdom in battle dress. I had found it rolled up in my tin trunk. No doubt my former batman, Driver Lane, who had been with me for three years before I had been posted away from my company by an exasperated Commanding Officer, to wander round Italy like one of the lost tribes whose services no one wanted, had bundled it up and put it there. And Driver Lane was possibly one of the worst batmen who ever served in the Middle East or Italy. But he had been my friend. More important, he had been my banker. He had made a deep study of the Black Market and, while he had been with me, never had I to wonder where the next handful of banknotes, no matter of what denomination, was coming from.

I had just poured my first glass of Frascati and was sniffing it in the approved style, when I became conscious of someone standing in the aisle of the plane staring at me. I looked up, and saw a large man with the insignia of a Brigadier on his shoulders smiling at me. Being in a somewhat frivolous mood as a result of my release from nervous tension, I raised my glass and said,

"Good health, Brigadier."

"Michael Nelson, isn't it?" he said. "I would very much appreciate a glass, Michael. There's nothing aboard this damned craft. It's as bad as the American Navy."

Seeing that he knew my name, I indicated that he should take the seat opposite me, and proceeded to offer him a glass.

"You haven't placed me yet, have you?" he said. "Jack Harwood ..."

"I've got it. I knew you when you commanded one of the Queen's Battalions. Took you in and out of the line in my trucks. Made a dreadful balls of it one night and drove a load of your chaps into the arms of the enemy. Thank God none of them was killed."

"It was a misty night, Michael."

"Come off it, Brigadier, I was pissed out of my mind."

"Well, you did have quite a reputation in the Brigade. But let's draw a discreet veil over that. By the way, do you mind if I ask my General to join us? I know it's a liberty, but I'm sure he would appreciate it."

"I should be proud to offer you both the hospitality of the Royal Army Service Corps," I said, thanking my good luck that I had taken the precaution of packing a hamper with sufficient wine and food to feed at least six people.

The Brigadier departed and returned with a General, whom he introduced to me as Dickie. I don't know to this day whether it was his surname or his Christian name, but I decided to play safe and called him General.

"So what's your game?" asked the Brigadier.

Thinking it inappropriate to inform a Brigadier of all the rackets I had been up to during the last year in Italy, I contented myself with telling him and the General that I was on my way to be demobilized.

I noticed that the General had been eyeing the pâté on the seat beside him.

"Help yourself, General," I said. "The bread's not bad at all, but I'm afraid there's no butter. There are several kinds of cold meat, and I think you will appreciate the flavour of the tomatoes. I'm sorry about the wine. Just a little bit on the warm side. Perhaps you would prefer a glass of the red. It's not a bad Orvieto."

The General looked at the Brigadier in amazement.

"Here am I, Jack, on an R.A.F. Dakota, dying of thirst and starving to death, and you conjure up a young Captain of the Royal Army Service Corps like manna from Heaven."

I preened with pride. Happening to look along the aircraft I noticed a change on the faces of those gentlemen who had only a few minutes previously been looking at me with contempt.

The General savoured the pâté.

"Quite delicious," he pronounced.

He sipped the Frascati.

"Yes, I agree it could be one degree cooler."

Then turning to the Brigadier, he said, "We can't let this genius go, Jack, he must come with us to Berlin."

"Now, now, wait a minute," I said hurriedly. "Let's get one thing straight. I'm on my way to dear old England after five and a half long years of soldiering, four of them overseas, during which I have avoided death, maiming and Court Martial. I have no intention of doing anything else except collecting my demob suit and getting back into dear old Civvy Street."

"My dear boy, Civvy Street can offer you nothing."

"The Army has offered me nothing," I countered. "Except years of boredom, frustration, and being kicked around."

The Frascati must have been topping up the alcohol in my bloodstream, for I added, "Do you realize, General, how easy it is to go for years in the Army without being appreciated? If the High Command had listened to me, Alamein would not have gone off at half-cock, and the desert could have been cleared of the Hun in half the time it took Monty. In Italy, Salerno would not have been the near-disaster it was, and as for Churchill's utter folly of insisting on that landing at Anzio, I would not so much as have considered it."

I was nevertheless overcome by curiosity.

"Anyway, what's all this about Berlin?"

"Very simple, Michael. The General and I are proceeding to Berlin and joining our Headquarters in the British sector. Now, what about it? Why not come with us?"

I began to laugh.

"What's so funny about that?" asked the General. "I suppose you don't believe it can be arranged."

"Oh yes, I do. Anything can be arranged on the Old Boy network in the British Army," I said. "No, what's so funny, after all these long years when no one has appreciated my genius, is that on the very day that I am on my way to be demobbed, along come a General and a Brigadier who can appreciate my true value. But, gentlemen, you are making a mistake. Even if I should consider your offer for one moment, which I never would, you should know something about me. I'm a crook and the worst soldier in the British Army, who took over four years to reach the rank of Captain, which I believe is a record in wartime. I detest discipline and restriction. I'm a coward and a drunkard. Here, let's open this second bottle of Frascati, and you can drink to my success in Civvy Street."

I produced a corkscrew attached to the end of my lanyard. Seeing the General watching me, and imagining that he might disapprove of my using my lanyard for such a practical purpose, I said, "I know it's meant to have a whistle on the end, General, but I lost it years ago. I wasn't even quite sure why I needed a whistle in the first place. But I do know that we wear our lanyards on the left in the Corps on account of the act of incredible bravery of some drivers who went in and pulled out some guns in the face of the enemy. If you ask my opinion, they must have been boozed up to the eyebrows."

"No, no, dear boy," said the General, "I wasn't being in the least critical. I was admiring your foresight. Many's the good bottle that has been ruined for the lack of a corkscrew. They should be carried at all times."

"Like prophylactics," I said.

"Exactly, like prophylactics. As you are aware, in the trousers of your battle dress is a little pocket especially built in to hold a small object to protect a soldier from the diseases of Venus."

"Must we, General?" said the Brigadier, who was about to place a slice of pâté between his lips.

Ignoring him, the General continued: "Do you realize, Captain, that during the Italian Campaign, there were permanently two divisions of Allied troops incapacitated through their failure to make use of that little object? I would have made it a Court Martial offence for any soldier to be found without one."

"I would have opened brothels and had them medically inspected by the Royal Army Medical Corps," I said.

"You underestimate the power of the Establishment. The Church would never have stood for it," said the General. "Perhaps you didn't know that they were responsible for the closing of the brothels in Alexandria and Cairo, and those brothels were well organized. One for the men, one for the N.C.O.s, and one for the Officers."

"You are referring to Mary's House, of course," I said. "Many were the happy hours I passed in dalliance there. But don't let's be so sordid. Here am I returning to the arms of the English roses only to be reminded of my squalid past."

"English roses be buggered," said the Brigadier.

I did not at the time appreciate the significance of the Brigadier's language.

"I'm afraid you're going to find the Old Country changed," said the General. "I hope you're not going to be disappointed."

"You've seen quite a bit of it since the war?"

"Oh, yes, I've been flying backwards and forwards for consultations at the War Office for the last six months."

"Some Generals have all the luck," I said. I was about to complain bitterly of the way I had been detained in Italy against my will, but thought better of it. It would have been churlish to have started to moan in such excellent company. Instead, I opened a parcel of cold quails.

From the exclamations of admiration and appreciation from my companions, I knew that, had it been within their power to promote me Major on the spot, they would not have hesitated.

At the end of the meal I apologized for the lack of coffee and cigars, but luckily I was able to produce a bottle of brandy.

"I'm sorry it's not French," I said. "But I think you will agree it's the best that Italy can produce."

I poured the General a generous measure. He sipped it and nodded.

"Not at all bad. Not at all bad. Oh, I wish you had run my Mess for me back in Italy. Where did you get it?"

"From the Mafia," I said. The effects of the drink were overcoming me, and, as soon as I had spoken, I knew I must watch my tongue.

"The Mafia? What do you mean?" said the Brigadier.

"Just a figure of speech, you know," I said. "You know, under the counter."

"You mean the Black Market, of course," said the General.

"That's right. The very Black Market," I said. "Now let me fill your glasses up."

The plane started to descend.

"Taking on fuel," commented the Brigadier. "Shall we alight on landing and stretch our legs?"

"Why spoil a pleasant party?" said the General.

"Absolutely," I agreed. "Look, gentlemen, I am going to place the brandy against the seat, and would you kindly pour your own in future."

"A Captain of unappreciated genius," murmured the General. "Can I ask you once more, Captain, to come with me to Berlin?"

"In no way, General. I am going back to Civvy Street. Captain Blossom returns to Civvy Street."

"Captain Blossom? I thought you were Michael Nelson."

I explained to the General and the Brigadier the origin of the name Captain Blossom. How, during my month's leave in England a year before, I had caught sight of myself in a glass and noticed that my face was streaked with red blotches, and had recalled how Joseph Conrad in one of his books had called these alcoholic scars Grog Blossoms. In my drunken stupor, feeling rather sad at the time, I had placed my fingers on them and said to myself, "What a mess you're in, Captain Blossom."

It was one of the best parties I have ever had in a plane. We discussed the war, we evaluated the Generals, admirals, and politicians. And, although I was of very junior rank to my fellow travellers, I was aware of the activities and failures of many of the people we discussed.

"Talking about failures," said the General, "the other day I ran into a very senior Officer, and I mentioned a fellow General, let's call him Boofy, who had been at Staff College with me. 'Boofy, Boofy?' said the Very Senior Officer. 'Oh yes. A grand fellow. Know him well. Lost an Armoured Brigade in the Desert.

Splendid chap.' "

It seemed to me at the time unfair that some people could get away with losing an armoured brigade, but if I had been caught flogging a few gallons of petrol or a handful of rations, I would have been clapped in irons.

I fell asleep and it was not until we came into land in England that the Brigadier gave me a shake. I noticed that the debris of our meal had all been neatly packed back into the hamper. I leaned forward, feeling very much the worse for wear, and poured myself a large brandy.

"Either of you care for a drink?" I asked. "Thank-you for tidying up. You need not have bothered. I thought I'd leave the rest of the food and the booze to the crew in appreciation of a safe journey."

"Please yourself," said the Brigadier. "But I'd hang on to it if I were you. Drink's difficult to come by in the Old Country at the moment."

"Been a war on, you know," said the General.

"I do know," I replied.

"I don't think the Captain knows what we're talking about, Jack," said the General.

"There's been a war on, Michael," said the Brigadier, almost shouting.

"Don't let's fall out over a hamper," I said. "You can take it, for all I care."

Before the Brigadier could lay hands on it, the General had grabbed it up and placed it firmly on his lap.

"First come, first served, Jack," he said.

"You're pulling rank," said the Brigadier, sounding peeved.

As we taxied across the airfield, I peered through the small windows. The sun was shining. In the distance I could see a bank of green trees. It was a perfect summer's day. Just the kind of day that I had dreamed for years would greet me on my return. I swallowed my brandy and sighed in anticipation. I was happy, if drunk.

The plane came to a halt. The General, clutching the hamper, moved up the aisle towards the door, with the Brigadier and me behind him, while the rest of the planeload of Officers waited respectfully for us to pass. Even in my somewhat dazed condition, I could not help noticing that I was coming in for a considerable amount of close scrutiny.

The door was opened. A ladder was placed in position. The

General, clutching his hamper, descended on to the ground. The Brigadier followed him. It was now my turn.

I negotiated the ladder to the one but bottom rung. Unfortunately I did not notice there was one left. I stumbled and fell flat on my face. Luckily for me, we had landed on a grass runway. Had it been tarmac, it is possible that after all those years of soldiering without damage, I might have injured myself.

As I lay on my face, the sweet smell of English grass pervaded my nostrils. I do not know what overcame me. Possibly some primitive emotion like love of my homeland. But before I could stop myself I started to kiss the turf of my beloved England.

The General and the Brigadier behaved like the great gentlemen they were. Solemnly, without a word, they knelt down on either side of me and did the same. Then, both placing an arm under me, they raised me to a standing position and marched me to a waiting car.

A corporal held open the rear door, and the General and the Brigadier assisted me into a corner seat. The General got in beside me; the Brigadier took the front seat next to the Corporal.

Through the front window I noticed the pennant of a two-star General flying on the bonnet. I turned and looked through the rear window. Officers were descending from the plane. Those already on the ground had come to attention and were saluting the General. This was the first time I had ever been in a car that had been saluted. I made a supreme effort and sat upright on the rear seat and raised my hand to my peaked cap, in the most casual manner that I could muster. I wanted it to look as if it was an action I had been accustomed to a thousand times or more.

"War Office, sir?" said the Corporal.

"No, Aldershot. We'll drop the Captain first at the Demob Barracks."

The Corporal let in the clutch. We moved slowly across the field, gathering speed. At the gate the guards presented arms. There was no delay, no formality.

Before I fell asleep I took one more look over the Corporal's shoulder at the flapping pennant, and sighed deeply. How I would have enjoyed being a General.

Two hours later we drove into the barracks at Aldershot. I thanked the General and the Brigadier for their courtesy in delivering me. They in turn thanked me for the food and drink I have been able to supply on the flight. It was a brief farewell. I had learnt in the army to accept the fact that one could be thrown together with agreeable companions for a few hours only, and that when the time came to part, one quickly and quietly went about one's own business.

I got out of the car, came to attention, and threw up the best salute of which I was capable. The General and the Brigadier touched their red-banded caps in a way that I now knew that I would never achieve.

As the car drove out of the barracks I noticed that my hamper was still on the back seat next to the General and he had a proprietary hand resting on it. I saw the sentries on the Main Gate present arms. I made my way into the barracks and presented myself to the Reception Officer, who did not seem at all pleased to meet me. Clearly he did not like the look of me, or maybe it was the state of my uniform that upset him. Then, feeling somewhat weary after the journey, having been informed that I would not be demobbed until the next morning, I made my way to my billet. It was bare and nasty. It contained two iron bedsteads with decidedly used blankets on both. I chose the cleaner of the two, lay down and closed my eyes.

I was woken from a dream in which I was holding back a division of Germans with the aid of a pitchfork. I raised my head from the pillow only to feel as if someone was hitting it with a frying pan. I tried to open my mouth to protest, but there seemed to be some foul tasting gum inside it, so that all I could do was to let out a groan, and let my head fall back.

In the far distance I heard a voice say, "Not much change I can see. Still on the grog."

Although the voice was far away, I dimly recognized it. Making the supreme sacrifice, I made a second attempt to sit up and opened my eyes. When they had come into focus and the golden spots behind them had settled down, I let out a gasp of surprise which succeeded in ungluing my mouth.

For there, standing beside me, was my old friend John Fish, with whom I had soldiered—if I may be permitted to use the word—for four years on and off overseas; with whom I had fought—again if I may use the word—from Alamein to the Alps.

"John!" I croaked, "What on earth are you doing here?"

"Come to welcome you home, of course. Here. You look seedy. I expect you need a heart starter."

From the briefcase that he was carrying, John produced two

glasses and a bottle of Scotch, poured two measures, and handed me one.

"Seriously," I said, "what are you doing here?"

"I've told you. To welcome you back to the dear Old Country."

"But how did you know?"

"A friend at the War Office, Department Demob. Told him to keep a look-out for you when your number came up."

"You don't change, do you?" I said, remembering that John Fish was the great contact man, the perfect fixer of all times. If it was information he was after, he would obtain it; if it was booze or butter or caviare, John would produce it from the back of his truck. While Field Marshals would have traded in their batons for a glass of water, John would be opening a bottle of champagne, and vintage into the bargain.

As my eyes began to clear as a result of the remedial effects of the Scotch, I noticed that John had only three pips on his shoulder. I let out a cry of amazement. When I had last seen John in Italy he had risen to the rank of Lieutenant-Colonel, and through our days together he had always managed, admittedly with no difficulty, to stay one or two ranks above me. In fact, the one way I had been able to irritate him was to remind him that the army in many ways resembled a pomegranate because one got more pips by sucking.

Pointing at his shoulder, I said, "How are the mighty fallen, *Captain* Fish?"

"I knew that would give your infantile mind pleasure," said John. "I assume you know the war is over, or have you been too boozed up to take that in? It's quite simple. Wartime soldiers like you are being discharged by the million. As a result, regular soldiers who were promoted to higher ranks while we fought the common enemy no longer have vast armies to command, so we are all dropping rank right, left and center."

For the first time it dawned on me that it was odd that John, who had returned to England at least a year ago, should still be in the army.

"What on earth are you still doing playing soldiers?" I asked.

"I have signed on."

"You've bloody what?" I shouted. I was totally confused. For four years on and off we had talked of Civvy Street, of that happy day that lay in the unforeseeable future when we would be demobbed. Wherever we had been, guarding the oilfields in Iraq with one division when they were threatened by 120 German divisions on the other side of the Caucasus with only the Russians between them and us, in the bars of Cairo where the hostesses promised unmentionable delights but vanished like ghosts through walls at closing time, in the Black Market restaurants of Naples as we consumed Typhoid-giving oysters by the dozen, in places too many to recall, in situations too unmentionable, we had never ceased to talk of that day when we would step ashore in England and receive that piece of paper that every civilian soldier dreamed of nightly, his discharge paper.

"Now I've heard everything," I said, after the throb in my head had subsided. "Why on earth did we trouble to win the war?"

"That, my dear fellow, is exactly what you're going to ask yourself when you've been here only a few weeks," said John. "Let me tell you right now that you're not going to like what you see."

He leant forward and refilled my glass. Looking down at the bottle he said, "I suppose you think this is just ordinary whisky?"

"It tastes fine to me."

"It is *gold* water," said John.

I shook my head. "I don't understand."

"Where do you think it comes from?"

"A shop. The NAAFI."

"The Black Market. Seven pounds a bottle."

I whistled. "That's a bit steep."

"You're going to get a real dose of shell shock," said John. "You had better face up to the facts of life. This is the most horrible country."

"Come off it. This is God's country."

"If it ever was, God has seen fit to forsake it," said John.

"Don't go and spoil my day, John," I protested. "Come on, tell me the truth. What made you sign on?"

"Look, Michael. I don't want to depress you. This is as you say, your day. I felt the same as you do now when I came home a year ago. Luckily I came home a few months before I was due for my discharge. And what I saw I didn't like. So I changed my mind and decided to sign on for a year or two."

"You mean you couldn't face Civvy Street, you couldn't stand on your own feet. I always suspected you were perfect military material and really wanted to be molly-coddled from the cradle to the grave. That was always your trouble, John. You really liked the army discipline and not having to think for yourself."

"Those remarks are beneath contempt and not worthy of you," said John.

I knew he was speaking the truth. "I'm sorry. Forgive me if I'm a bit confused and shocked."

"Just keep your mouth shut," said John, "and keep your eyes open. And don't say I didn't warn you. Let's go across to the mess. Maybe there you will get the first step in your education."

I got off the bed, adjusted my battle dress to the best of my ability, and followed John in a state of mystification out of the billet and across the barrack square. On the way John stopped by a fifteen hundred weight truck and deposited his dispatch case, into which he had returned the bottle of whisky, inside the tool box, which he then proceeded to fasten with a padlock that would have made the Bank of England secure.

I wasn't at all happy about the Mess into which he led me. Its interior walls were daubed with brown paint which was flaking off; its floor covered by linoleum in which were large holes, which in my opinion were a serious hazard for anyone trying to negotiate them if somewhat the worse for drink; its furniture consisted of bare trestle tables, a few hard-backed chairs, and a sofa whose springs and stuffing were bursting out in all directions.

To ease the pain of these first impressions, I said "Let me buy you a drink John. Where's the bar?"

Smiling at me John pointed to a hole in the far corner.

"That's the serving hatch," I said.

John was still smiling. "That's the bar."

I hastened towards it. On its other side was a soldier in a white jacket reading the Daily Mirror. I knocked imperiously on the counter. "Two large Scotches, soldier," I said.

"Sir?" he said, putting down his paper and rising to his feet with no signs of hurry or enthusiasm, so that I could not help thinking if he had been one of my own merry men I would have given him a right bollocking then and there.

"Two large Scotches, soldier."

"No Scotch," he said. No doubt noticing the increasing colour in my cheeks, he added, "Sir."

"How bloody inefficient," I said. "How on earth you can allow yourself to run out in a demob Mess where we're all longing to celebrate, is beyond my comprehension."

"They all say that, Sir," he said shaking his head.

"Better make it two double gins then," I said.

He shook his head.

"What, no bloody gin either?" I said.

"Only allowed to serve singles ... Sir."

"Oh God, what bloody nonsense is this? Then make it four singles."

Again he shook his head. "A single gin only per Officer before your dinner, Sir."

I turned to John who was standing behind me. He was shaking with laughter.

"He's speaking the truth. One gin per Officer before dinner, and one per Officer afterwards. Give him your name, by the way, so that he can tick you off on his list."

I was too dumbfounded to speak. Without thought for the future, I seized my single gin and downed it in one gulp. "Well, let's get some dinner and go out and find a drink elsewhere."

"Do you fancy the menu?" asked John pointing at a piece of paper pinned up next to the hatch. I looked at it and read:

>Spam and mashed potatoes
>Tea

"There are some right comedians round here," I commented. "Now let's see the proper menu."

John shook his head and I detected a look of sorrow in his eyes. "That is the real menu, Michael."

"But I ate better than that when I was a driver at Inkermann Barracks in Woking in 1940," I said.

"That was before we started to fight the war," said John. He drank his gin. "Come on, let's go hunting and see what we can find."

"Ah, you haven't changed much, have you? I bet you know as usual where the best crumpet hangs out."

Again John sadly shook his head. "First things first. Booze to celebrate your homecoming, secondly something reasonable to eat."

I was silent as we left the Mess, walked across the square and got into John's truck. Silent, because I was depressed. My great day was getting off to a bad start. I had imagined myself popping bottles of champagne as I treated everyone in the Mess to a celebratory glass; I had dreamed of red steaks with salad; of English roses welcoming me with open arms and leading me to their beds whose sheets would be strewn with flowers in honour of the hero returning from the wars.

We drove out of Aldershot into the surrounding country. As usual John imagined that he was at the wheel of a racing car, and I was glad that there was not much traffic about, a fact which I remarked on.

"Of course there isn't, you twit. Didn't you know petrol was rationed?"

In my last year in Italy since the war I had read something about it. But I had been too occupied with my own problems and too infuriated with the army for retaining my services long after the war was over to pay much attention to what was happening in England.

We rounded a bend with tyres squealing, and there was the pub I had dreamed of for years. A thatched cottage with the sign of the Cat and Fiddle hanging outside. A perfect English inn with a warm welcome inside to travellers on a hot and thirst-making day in August.

John turned the wheel hard over, and with tyres protesting even more loudly we came to a halt in front of the oak door.

"Bugger," said John.

"What's the matter?" I asked.

"Can't you read, nit? Look, pinned to the door."

On a piece of paper, I read the words NO BEER.

I got out of the truck, went up to the door and pounded it with my fists.

"You're wasting your time," said John. "Come on, hop in. We may have to do a fair amount of mileage before we strike lucky."

We drove about twenty miles that evening. Everywhere we encountered the same sign. NO BEER. NO BEER.

On one occasion we found a mob queueing outside a pub.

"What on earth are they doing?" I asked.

John strode to the head of the queue. On all sides there were mutterings and threatening voices. Someone shouted "You're not in the army now. So don't pull your bloody rank, Captain."

John ignored the rabble and pointed to a notice on the door which read OPEN AT 9 P.M.

"Well, why don't we join in?" I asked in desperation.

"Because, my dear Michael, there's no guarantee that when it's our turn to be served, there will be any beer left."

"My God, to think that it should come to this," I said. For a moment my thoughts turned to Italy where, even if I had felt cheated, the wine had never ceased to flow; where the best hotels in the land had been glad of my custom. In particular, I remembered the Albergo Grande in Rome where I had spent two unbelievable nights with a blonde called Lucia who had been recommended to me by my batman as a girl of great accomplishments, and with whom I had eaten two pots of caviare washed down with the finest wines.

We returned to the truck where John sat thinking a minute. "There's only one thing for it. I must sell myself for you."

"What do you mean?" I asked.

"Wait and see."

Half an hour later we approached a nasty-looking road house not far from Guildford. There were no signs of life in front of it, and John swung off the road and drove round to the back where there were a dozen cars parked.

"At least they're open," he said.

The back door was locked and he pressed the bell with what sounded like a private signal. The bolts were drawn back and the door was opened by a very pretty-looking blonde, who immediately threw her arms round John and covered him with kisses. Seeing me she became hostile. "Who's that with you?" she asked suspiciously.

"A very old friend, Michael Nelson. Michael, this is Julia."

I stepped forward and bowed gallantly. "At your service, my dear lady."

She looked at me as if I was something to be avoided at all costs, put her arms round John and led him into the house. "Bolt the door behind you," she called to me without looking round.

I did as I was bid, and found my way back into the bar. The place was crowded, mostly with Americans and Canadians, with here and there a sprinkling of British. Julia had taken up her position behind the bar and was deep in conversation with John. A second barmaid was doing all the work, and I took my place in the queue waiting to be served by her. I could not help noticing that, to put it mildly, she was no beauty. To begin with, her hair could have done with a wash, and where there were teeth in her mouth, they were blackened. Nevertheless I could see that she had her followers, and some she clearly preferred to others. To those she favoured she was prepared to offer a smile and, to my utter astonishment, a full kiss on her lips, the constant kissing of which had smeared her lipstick so that it gave her the appearance of having a red moustache. Those who were out of favour were received with a blank stare and hurriedly served in dirty glasses with short measure into the bargain.

When my turn came I put on my best manner and said, "Two pints of beer, please Miss."

"Mrs, to you. And we only serve halves."

"And twenty Players."

"Them that don't say please gets nothing," she replied. "Anyway, we've got no fags in the place."

Remembering that I was with John, I said "Oh, and ask Captain Fish and his friend what they would like."

"You with him?"

I nodded.

"Then you can have a pint. The Captain will have a large whisky and her ladyship will have a large gin and tonic."

"Could you make mine a large Scotch too, please?" I asked.

"I'll have to ask her ladyship," she said. She sauntered along the bar and whispered in the ear of the girl who had been introduced to me as Julia. She came back to me and said "Yes, it's O.K."

"Make it a White Horse, then," I said.

"Bloody funny some of us are, aren't we?"

She poured the drinks and banged them on the bar.

"What'll you have, please?" I asked.

"That's better," she said. "The sooner some of us learn manners the better it will be for all of us."

I picked up John and Julia's drinks and was about to carry them along the bar to give to them, when my new-found friend shouted "Don't be a cunt and leave your whisky there, or some bugger will nick it and that's for sure."

Shaken by her language and her looks, I scooped up my own drink and went to join John and Julia. I gave Julia her gin and tonic, which she took without saying thank-you, swept away down the bar ignoring the clamouring customers, and stalked out of the room.

"What goes on here, for Christ's sake?" I asked.

"To put it bluntly, Julia thought I had come here to see her," said John. "She's not at all pleased I've brought you here to celebrate."

"Who the hell is she anyway?" I asked.

"She owns this charming establishment. Her old man died in the war."

"I'm sorry for anyone who is left a war widow, but I still don't like the way she looks at me."

"He died of cirrhosis," said John.

"You could have fooled me from what I've seen so far. Doesn't seem to be enough of the stuff about to get pissed on once."

"What you've got to understand, Michael, is that what matters today is to be a basic producer and provider. That's what counts today. That's what makes the money. It may interest you to know that Julia is well on her way to being a millionairess."

"Then why not marry her?"

"My dear Michael, now crude can you be? What is marriage without love?"

I was about to throw what remained of the Scotch in my glass into John's face but, in view of the shortage of the vital commodity in the Old Country, I desisted.

"However I have done the best for you under the circumstances. Because I have spoken up for you and presented your case with all the power at my command, she has agreed, if with a somewhat bad grace, that you shall dine with us. I trust that you will appreciate the sacrifice I am making on your behalf."

"Some sacrifice," I commented. Looking round the bar and seeing at least four men to every woman in the place, not to mention the queue that was still trying to curry favour with the black-toothed darling, I decided to cut my losses. Not for me on this night of my great day would there be an English rose. I would concentrate on getting thoroughly stoned.

After John had brought me another drink he looked at his watch. "Time to dine."

I followed him into the dining room where Julia was already seated on a banquette with her back to the wall. She pointed to the seat on her right for John to occupy, then turned to me and indicated that I should take the chair at the end of the table on her left. Having exhausted herself on my behalf, she turned her back on me and ignored me completely during the entire course of the meal.

I must confess that although the dinner was not the feast that I had promised myself on my first day back in England, it was at least edible and preferable to the disgraceful menu pinned up back at the demob barracks. But I have always been the kind of person who thinks that food and conversation go well together, and having to sit there and talk to myself was boring in the extreme. It was particularly irritating because John seemed to be enjoying Julia's company and I could hardly fail to observe his hand frequently straying beneath the tablecloth. The only thing to be said in favour of the evening was that the waiter kept replenishing my glass as soon as it was empty. It was very good wine, if I remember correctly, a pre-war claret, but it was not until I happened to notice Julia raise her little finger and point it in my direction, whereupon the waiter once again refilled my glass, that I realized she was trying to get me tight.

So that's your little game, I thought. You little bitch, trying to come between me and my old mate John Fish. So you want me out of the way, do you?

I leant across her, and said "John, I think we ought to be on our way. If you remember I have to report to barracks before midnight."

John looked surprised. "Aren't you happy or something? Not getting enough to drink?"

"It's just that duty calls," I said.

"It's never called before," said John. "I wonder why it should for the first time tonight?"

I rose, if somewhat unsteadily, from the table. "Come, Captain Fish ..."

"Just bloody well sit down and keep quiet," interrupted Julia.

But I was not to be silenced on my first night in England. "My dear lady, I ..."

"Don't bloody well 'dear lady' me," she shouted. Turning to John, she added "Will you tell your friend to piss off out of it."

Sensing that everyone else in the dining room was watching our table, and not wishing to be the cause of a vulgar confrontation with Julia, even if she was not a lady, I could see that the moment had come for a strategic retreat. In other words, I knew that I was beaten; that I was no match for Julia. Beneath that beautiful blonde exterior, I could detect an interior of steel, not to mention an expertise with a nail file which I had no desire to encounter.

To my amazement John stood up. "It is true," he said, "duty does call."

Julia was taken off balance. "What's the game? What are you two up to?"

"Nothing, my love," said John. He took out his wallet and tossed a handful of fivers on the table.

The sight of them had quite the opposite effect to what I imagined. Grabbing up the notes, Julia hurled them on the floor.

"I don't want your filthy money," she screamed at the top of her voice.

I was about to kneel down to retrieve the notes, never liking to see the stuff thrown away, when John grabbed me by the arm and hurried me towards the door. "Time to beat a retreat I feel."

I needed no encouragement. We were out of the dining room, along the passage, through the front door, into the truck and roaring away before Julia had time to rally her strength and attack. For the first time, I began to laugh. Our withdrawal had been beautifully executed, timed to perfection. It was gratifying that, although we had not had to put it into action together for over a year, the art had not deserted us. It was a technique that we had perfected in the dives and dosshouses of the Middle East. It had stood us good stead in Naples, it had extracted us from the ugliest situations in the back streets of Rome. Fundamentally it was a question of making a quick decision. The principles were the same as those of attack. If you're going to attack, do so with all your strength and do not dilly-dally on the way. When retreat is unavoidable, withdraw with a swiftness and suddenness that will leave your enemy off balance. By the time he recovers, you are out of range.

As we drove back in the direction of the barracks, I said "Tell me, John, what decided you to leave with me? She's not my type, but I can quite see she might have some attraction for certain people."

"Not your type! You mean you couldn't bloody well get near her."

"I've seen enough violence in the last four years," I said, "I have no intention of dying on the end of a nail file on my first night home. You haven't answered my question. Why did you desert the blonde bombshell?"

"What you saw tonight was nothing. It is very simple really. She cannot survive without a row. She must have a row with someone every evening. I suspect she obtains some kind of sexual excitement from it."

"In my opinion, after tonight you can wave goodbye to her for ever," I said.

"Nonsense, she needs me. And not in the sense your dirty mind is thinking of. Shall I say that I am able to help her to run a successful business in these times of desperate shortage." He took one hand off the wheel and held it up. "I shall say no more and expect no questions."

Half an hour later we turned into the barracks and John halted the truck outside the Mess, went to the tool box and took out a bottle of whiskey. "Time for a nightcap, I feel," he said and led the way in.

There were half a dozen Officers sitting about in various stages of dejection, and I assumed that all the others had given up in desperation in this desert of a room and gone to bed. What a way to spend your last night in the army, I thought.

John went to the hatch, disturbed the steward, and demanded the remaining ration of gin. The Officers watched him anxiously, and smiles of relief lit up their faces when he returned with the gins and a tray of empty glasses which he put on the table with the bottle of whiskey.

"Gentlemen," he announced, "You don't know how lucky you all are to be here in this desert of a Mess on the eve of your release from service to His Majesty. Michael is a very old friend of mine, and it is my intention to float him out of the army through which he has swum for the last five years or more. So help yourselves."

They all held back, none of them wishing to appear too eager, although each of them had a tongue hanging out.

John picked up the bottle and filled the glasses. "I have some more outside in the truck," he said.

"John, you're a genius," I said. "I don't know how I could have fought through those dangerous years without you at my side."

"Fought? I think the correct word is survived. When I think of the number of times I came between you and a Court Martial, my mind boggles."

"The only thing that ever came between you and me were members of the opposite sex," I said. "It was the same tonight. Julia was the only decent one in the place, if a bit handy with the nail file."

"There was that charmer behind the bar for you, wasn't there? Some people want jam on it all the time."

"I thought her tooth might give me blood poisoning," I said.

It was a very good party that night. I forgot the earlier disappointments of the evening, the horrible sight of all those public houses with their No Beer signs stuck to their doors, the absence of an English rose to welcome me home. I was able to recount with considerable success my encounter with the General and the Brigadier on the plane. There were a few doubting Thomases who refused to believe me, until a Major who had been on the same aircraft was able to confirm my story.

I am happy to say that not one of us became maudlin. We did, as was only to be expected, recall old places and faces. But in each one of us was a sense of excitement, a feeling of gratitude, that this day for which we had prayed so hard and often, had finally come. Tomorrow we would be civilians again.

It was after John had given his rendering of "There Once Was a Gay Caballero," that the trouble started.

Our rendering of this fine old ballad was followed by one of the party with an excellent voice giving us his version of "Please Don't Burn My Shithouse Down."

This prompted me to declare in a loud voice that Aldershot was a disgrace, the demob barracks a scandal, and the Mess in which we were now celebrating worse than a shithouse and fit only for the flames.

My remarks were greeted on all sides with enthusiasm, and in a few minutes we had all the furniture, the sofa with its stuffing hanging out, the bare trestle tables, and anything else we could lay our hands on or tear from the walls heaped up in a pyramid in the center of the room.

After that there was nothing more to do. It was a fitting climax to the party, and bidding one another good-night we stumbled out into the night wishing one another good luck, knowing that we should never meet again.

"Are you sure you're all right?" said John. "Sure you don't want me to conduct you back to your billet?"

"I'm completely in control. Have you ever seen me otherwise?"

"On occasions too numerous to relate," he replied. "Right. See you in the morning before I get back to my unit."

"Thanks for the party," I said.

I watched him march off across the square, which was lit by a dozen arc lamps which seemed to me a waste of the taxpayers' money at that time of the night. From the main gate there came the sound of commands. No doubt it was the changing of the guard.

To this day I do not know what got into me. Maybe it was the effect of the fresh air on the drink. Maybe I'm a secret pyromaniac. But some force compelled me to walk back to the Mess we had just left. I pushed open the door. The lights were still on and there in the center of the room was that heap of furniture piled up to the ceiling. Maybe memories of childhood flooded into me, and I was back at home on November 5, waiting for my mother and father to come out and light the bonfire. Whatever it was, I was stricken by an irresistible urge.

I had to set fire to that pile of furniture. I had no choice. It was inevitable.

I felt an intense dislike for the piece of paper on the wall, the so-called menu, Spam and Mashed Potatoes, Tea. I crossed the room, and there it was, that offensive scrap of paper that had escaped the general carnage. I tore it off the wall and crumpled it in my hand.

In a trance I returned to the pile of furniture. That abomination of a menu should be the first to go, I told myself. I took out my lighter and set fire to it. As soon as it was well alight I stuck it under the stuffing of the sofa which was at the bottom of the heap. It took fire beautifully with a bluish flame, that rapidly increased in intensity, taking hold of a broken wicker paper basket that was sitting on top of it.

I stood back, studied my handiwork with pleasure, turned on my heel and walked out of the Mess, not forgetting to close the door behind me.

As I walked in a soldierly manner across the square, I felt that I had exorcized something out of my soul. What it was I do not know. Perhaps this act of pyromania was a kind of catharsis. I was, or so I thought at the time, a civilian once again. All my hatred, all frustrations brought on by the military life, were going up in flames behind me.

As I lay my head on the greasy pillow in my billet and pulled a dirty blanket over my body, I thought I heard the sound of a fire engine in the far distance. I did not care. Those bells were sweet music in my ears.

I was awakened by a loud banging on my door. The door opened. A Sergeant came in and saluted.

"Captain Nelson, Sir?"

"Yes."

"You're to report to the Adjutant's Office immediately, Sir."

He saluted, turned about smartly and left the billet, crashing the door behind him.

I struggled out of bed, went to the basin and shaved myself. I dressed and smartened myself up to the best of my ability, and stepped out into a perfect August day.

I looked around the square in the happy knowledge that this was my last morning in the army.

I stopped in my tracks as in the far corner I saw a charred ruin of a hut that had been cordoned off with white ropes. At the same time I saw John striding across the square in my direction, in immaculate service dress.

"You silly bugger," he said when he reached me. "It was you, wasn't it? For Christ's sake keep your big mouth shut and say as little as possible, or it won't be a demob for you but a Court Martial and a couple of years inside."

I felt ill. I thought I was going to vomit. I had heard fire bells. Yes, of course it had been me. I could see that wretched menu burning, the hair coming out of the chair taking light, and the flames licking upwards.

"Now listen, Michael," said John as we walked across the square. "They know we were the last to leave. What on earth made you go back and do such a bloody silly thing? Oh, it doesn't matter. I don't suppose you will ever be able to tell me. Anyway we haven't time now to go into all that."

"How do they know we were the last to leave?"

"The Reception Officer on his way to his own billet saw us on the square chatting before we said good-night."

"That's bad."

"Of course it's bloody bad. Anyway, I suppose I've got to perjure myself once again on your behalf. I'm going to say I saw you back to your billet. Get it? And you never went near the place after I left you there."

The Orderly Sergeant was waiting for us. "The Adjutant would like to see you right away, gentlemen. Would you please go in."

We went in, came to attention and saluted.

"I suppose you know what I want to see you about?"

"No, Sir," snapped John.

"And you, Captain Nelson?"

"No, Sir."

"How very surprising," said the Adjutant.

He had not asked us to stand at ease. I could sense he was one of those sarcastic buggers who like to keep his victims dancing on the edge of a string for as long as possible.

"Then you didn't notice anything different about the barracks this morning?"

"Yes, Sir," said John, "the demob Officers' Mess appears to have been gutted by a fire last night."

"And you, Captain Nelson?"

"No, Sir. I mean yes, Sir."

"Well, what do you mean, Captain Nelson?"

"I did hear some fire bells last night, Sir. A very bad business, if I may say so, Sir."

This was stupid of me. There was no point in aggravating the Adjutant further. I could feel John stiffen beside me in annoyance. Flippancy has always been one of my strong suits and has never got me anywhere.

"You realize, Captain Nelson, that this will mean we may have to detain you here for some time to take part in a Court of Enquiry." He paused ominously. "The result of the Court of Enquiry will naturally determine what Officer or Officers shall face Court Martial."

I was frightened. I think the Adjutant could sense it too. "There can be absolutely no excuse for any Officer behaving this way. Arson, and especially arson where it concerns His Majesty's property, is a most serious crime. I understand that those found guilty can be imprisoned for anything up to seven years."

"Oh, my God." I said softly.

"You spoke, Captain Nelson?"

"No, Sir."

"Anyway, gentlemen, I now propose to take you in to meet the Commanding Officer." He paused and added "I regret you will not be meeting him in happier circumstances."

He rose from his desk, crossed the room, and knocked on an adjoining door. Faintly, for I was gradually being overcome by shock, I heard a voice call "Come in."

John touched me on the shoulder. Together we marched into the Commanding Officer's room, came to attention and saluted.

As I have explained, I was suffering from a severe case of shock, with the result that my eyes had gone out of focus. In the distance I heard a voice say "Stand at ease, gentlemen."

I thought I recognized the voice. I forced my eyes to act properly on my behalf. Sitting behind the desk, eyeing me sternly, was my old friend Major Ben Lyons, the only difference being that he now carried the insignia of a Half Colonel on his shoulders.

I should explain here that soon after the end of the war in Italy, during the course of many postings, I had been sent to a General Transport Company in Bari commanded by a dreadful ex-ranker called Major Taylor, who eventually died in the most suspicious circumstances. His command had been taken over by Major Ben

Lyons, who had served with the Hussars where he had won an M.C. He would have liked to have taken a regular commission with the regiment, but had no private income and so had been unable to do so. Accordingly he had applied for and been accepted as a regular with the R.A.S.C. It had been Ben Lyons who had obtained my Captaincy for me after I had been a Lieutenant for over four years. I greatly respected him for having been the only Officer in the entire British Army to appreciate my true potential.

Ben Lyons looked at the Adjutant and said "Thank you. I will call you in when I need you."

The Adjutant seemed surprised, sprang to attention, saluted and marched out of the room.

"I wondered if it was the same Michael Nelson," said Ben Lyons. "Glad to see you. Just about a year ago, isn't it, since we last met?"

"That's right, Sir."

"And Captain Fish. I don't think we've met before. Of course, I've heard of you. Well now, what are we going to do about this little spot of bother?"

"I'm terribly sorry, Sir ..." I began.

"Nothing to be sorry about, Michael. These barracks were condemned long ago and, as I said to one of the Quartermaster General's Staff only a week ago, the electrical wiring is a positive menace."

"Ah yes, Sir. The electrical wiring, Sir," said John.

I could feel myself coming out of my state of shock. "Oh, thank-you, Ben," I said. "... Oh yes, that electrical wiring. God bless you, Ben. I mean the wiring."

"Feeling all right, Michael?" said Ben.

"A great deal better than I did two minutes ago."

"Just to be serious one minute, Michael. When you leave here, you're to proceed at once to the demob department, get kitted out and then fuck off out of here before I have you arrested." He paused. "And when you're safely back in Civvy Street, but not a day before, you will give me a call and come down and dine with me."

"I'm afraid Michael's going to get the shock of his life in Civvy Street, Colonel," said John. "I feel he's going to be very disappointed."

"You a regular?" asked Ben.

"I'm staying on for a few years. I was trying to persuade Michael to do the same, but the silly bugger won't listen to me."

Ben shook his head. "Not a chance, Captain. The army wouldn't have him."

"Look here, if they'll have John, they'll have me," I protested. "Not that I have any intention of staying in the sodding army."

"See what I mean, Colonel," said John. "The bloody fool thinks Civvy Street will be all roses and violets." Then he added somewhat maliciously, "But why wouldn't the army have him, Colonel?"

"I'm afraid it's a confidential matter."

"I'm not afraid to hear the truth," I said, somewhat irritated that after all my years of service, His Majesty should have the nerve to decline my services, even though I had not the slightest intention of offering them to him.

"Well, shall we say that the reports on him as a young Officer were not altogether—how shall I put it—satisfactory. As Michael knows, I had a hell of a job persuading H.Q. in Naples to make him up to Captain. There was one factor that especially went against him. An unfortunate occurrence in Naples after he returned from Anzio. But perhaps we should gloss over that."

"No, no, Ben, I can stand the truth."

"Well, er, there was that business of V.D.N.Y.D."

"Oh, you mean Michael got the clap," said John.

"That's a bloody lie," I said. "You know perfectly well it stands for V.D. Not Yet Diagnosed. In fact the tests were negative."

"That's what you say," said John. "But I have to admit she wasn't a bad-looking bit at all."

"And then there was the unfortunate episode of your striking the Lance Corporal in the Military Police when your Brigade had been sent back from Italy to refit in Alexandria. Do you want me to go on?" said Ben Lyons.

"I don't see the point," I said. "First of all it is all prejudiced evidence. Secondly, if you gave me a million pounds I wouldn't stay an hour more than it is necessary in the army."

Ben Lyons stood up. "Good luck to you both," he said, holding out his hand. "Ask the Adjutant to come in on your way out." He winked. "I must get him to put in another report on the adverse condition of the electrical wiring throughout the camp."

When we had come out of the Orderly Room onto the square, John let out a long sigh and wiped his brow.

"You realize how bloody lucky you are?" he said. "You know what saved you?"

"The Old Boy network. If Ben Lyons hadn't been in command, the situation could have proved decidedly dicey."

"You can say that again. May I suggest you take the Colonel's advice and fuck off before you get into really hot water. Here, let me give you my address."

He took out a notebook and wrote down the name and location of his company.

"Right, be seeing you."

"See you soon," I said.

With no further formality, no shaking of hands, he turned on his heel and marched in a soldierly manner across the square. On the far side he turned and called out "Good luck in Civvy Street. You'll bloody well need it."

# 2

"Two pants, short; two vests, string; two shirts; two collars, detachable; one suit, brown; one hat, Trilby; one shoes, black; one coat, over; two socks, wool; sign here, Sir, and good luck to you," said the Sergeant Quartermaster in a weary voice.

I could not help recalling the day in April 1941 when the difference had been that the voice had been loud and menacing as various items of military equipment had been hurled at me. I remembered one unfortunate conscript complaining that nothing fitted. "Then fucking well grow or fucking well shrink," the seargeant had bellowed.

I went into one of the cubicles and stripped off. Now was the moment of truth. A civilian at last. I took off my khaki shirt and put on the collarless shirt. Today, these are almost museum pieces. One only sees them worn by the elderly members of the working class. But before the war they were the universal badge of that class, usually worn without a collar and done up at the front with a stud.

When I had climbed into my suit I did not like one little bit what I saw in the mirror. The suit was on the stiff side, and must have contained a quantity of wood pulp. With the Trilby on my head, I could have passed for a Russian politician. Whichever way I looked at myself the result was disastrous. I had no choice. I undressed and redonned my uniform. I put my civilian outfit in a large cardboard box which the army had supplied with foresight. The army must have known that the shock would be too much for a great many people. Half an hour later, I was on the lorry to Aldershot station, with a rail pass to London in my pocket.

It was midday when I wandered along the platform seeking the buffet where I could obtain some light refreshment, as my summons to the Orderly Room had left me no time for breakfast. When I tracked it down it was no credit to Aldershot. Most of its windows were broken and not a daub of paint had been applied to its exterior for several years. I pushed open the door and marched in.

Several soldiers were sitting about drinking tea. There was a peculiar smell about the place. I could not identify it immediately, but after a few seconds reflection I decided that it was a mixture of dog, cat, and human urine. I walked to the bar on which a rusty tea urn was emitting clouds of steam. Behind it, filling a tin teapot with hot water, was an elderly lady dressed in black.

Before I could say anything, she pushed a cup containing a greyish liquid towards me and said "Twopence."

"No tea, thank you. I wonder if you could supply me with a large Scotch, please?"

"Another bloody comedian," she said. "Twopence, I haven't got all bloody day."

"Nor have I, madam," I replied. "I would be most grateful if you would be so kind as to let me have a large whiskey, please."

This perfectly polite request produced an unwarranted outburst. The lady to whom I had addressed my order leant across the counter and seized hold of my tie.

"I know your sort," she shouted. "Don't think I don't know about people like you. Got the bloody Africa Star and the bloody Wop medal haven't you? Think that entitles you to lord it around here, doesn't it?"

"No, madam ..."

"Think you can walk in here giving yourself airs and graces," she continued, ignoring my attempt to defend myself. "We know all about your type out there, having it away with the Negresses and whores, while we was being bombed to death with doodlebugs. Guzzling yourselves to death on best beef and gravy, while we had to make do here with a crust of bread if we were lucky."

She ran out of steam and loosened her hold on my tie.

"I gather there is no whiskey," I said, standing back from the bar in case this remark should result in a further onslaught on my person.

She looked at me and shook her head. "Haven't you got any bloody eyes in your head? There's bugger all here, is there?"

I looked along the shelves behind the bar, and her words confirmed my worst suspicions. All the bottles were empty. They had been empty a long time. They were covered with dust.

As I went out one of the soldiers touched me on the arm. "Just home, Sir?" I nodded.

"Don't get too depressed, Sir. It's not like this everywhere. Most stations are dry except in London and the big cities. You'll soon get the hang of it. Good luck, Sir."

A few minutes later I boarded a First class compartment and was on my way to Waterloo. Officers in those days only travelled First class and the rest of the forces went Third, as Second class had ceased to exist. When the railways were nationalized the bureaucrats in charge could not stand this charming anomaly, abolished Third and reintroduced Second class. This process of making the country conform to the norm has continued. And the profiteers will rub their hands with glee as everything is adjusted upwards.

As I sat staring out of the window my spirits rose. Although the Home Counties are not exactly the jewels of the English countryside, it was pleasing to see how little they had changed. It was a hot afternoon in August. The harvest was in progress, a great deal of it being carried in on carts. I was of course in a steam train, and now and again clouds of smoke curled past my window against the blue sky. In spite of the few initial setbacks, I found myself planning my first evening back in London. I would go to the Ritz. It seemed reasonable to suppose, if there was anywhere I could find a decent drink, it would be there. I might even take a room there for a few days while I had a look around London.

As we came into the outskirts of London I was able to study for the first time the effects of the bombings. It was very patchy. Here there would be acres of devastation, and then nothing for quarter of a mile, except for the odd house or two which I assumed must have been burned down by incendiaries. I was to discover later on that this pattern was repeated everywhere in the larger cities. In London, areas like the City and the Docks suffered badly. But the damage that was inflicted was nothing to that I had seen in Italy in a city like Naples. Nor of course had the British countryside suffered in the same way. No war had been fought over it, and accordingly complete villages and small towns had not been literally obliterated, as, for instance, had been Cassino, which had been reduced to square miles of rubbish with not a single building left standing.

I was so agreeably surprised to see so much of London still intact, if considerably more drab than it had done in 1939, that I alighted from the train at Waterloo in good heart. Although the station itself had been considerably knocked about, my good humour was increased when on visiting the bar and on demanding a whiskey I was given one without complaint.

While I sipped my drink, I looked round the bar and through the window at the main platforms. It was still a wartime scene. Men and women of all nations and of all branches of the services milled or lolled about in various stages of animation and exhaustion. The usual tannoy system gave out incomprehensible instructions. Between announcements military marches blared from the loudspeakers. It was a scene of considerable activity, and forgetting where I was, I downed the remains of my drink and asked for another one. "Make it a double," I said.

"Singles only."

I put my hand in my pocket and laid an half-crown on the bar. "I would like a double, please," I said, pushing the coin forward like a pawn on a chess board.

"Certainly, Sir. Coming up right away, Sir."

Looking back, this was a landmark in my return to Civvy Street. I was quickly to learn that in Britain after 1945 very little could be expected for nothing. This came as no kind of a shock to me. In the army this practice only partially applied. After all a command had to be obeyed, at least in the British army. In the American army there were areas where fair trading and bartering were permissible. For instance, I remember that John Fish had succeeded in trading six bottles of whiskey with the Americans in Naples in exchange for a Jeep. In fact it was even a better deal than that. The bottles had been opened and half filled with condensed water. The resealing had been carried out by a fitter of the Workshop Section who was highly skilled at this extra-mural activity. I like to think that he went far in civilian life.

When I say that the pushing forward of an half-crown piece in that bar on Waterloo station was a landmark, I should add that I started with a great advantage. For, dealing with the civilian population and the Black Marketeers in Italy, I had already perfected the art of "dropsy." No-one could exchange a note of the highest denomination with the skill that I had attained. It would glide from my palm into the hand of the recipient unperceived by even the most hawk-like eyes. Indeed there is a whole treatise to be written about the art of tipping and bribery. All I will do here is give would-be learners a word of warning. The great secret of tipping or bribery is discretion. Neither should be done openly. The man who openly tips a head waiter to secure a seat in a restaurant commits a grave error. He exposes that head waiter to charges of corruption. The sweetener should pass from hand to hand with a legerdemain worthy of a great illusionist.

Outside Waterloo station I encountered for the first time the sight of a real queue. It coiled away into the distance. It consisted mostly of servicemen loaded with pounds and pounds of heavy equipment. Now and again a single taxi would rumble up and a crowd would converge upon it. I discovered later that the taxi driver would pick up as many customers as possible going in the same direction, and charge each one of them the full fare. It must have been a profitable business to have owned a cab in those days.

Spurning the queue I set off across Waterloo Bridge in the direction of the Ritz Hotel. On the North Bank, Hitler's bombers had inflicted a modicum of damage. The Aldwych, the Strand, Trafalgar Square and Piccadilly were relatively untouched by bombs. They were still pleasant to look at, if somewhat drab. The destruction of London still lay in the future. But no doubt the gnomes in back rooms were already hatching their secret plans. Soon, brandishing their banners on which would be emblazoned the word DEVELOPMENT, they would be moving in. No place would be sacred. Nothing would be immune from them, acts of vandalism worthy of the Luftwaffe. In the forefront would march the University of London, which was to demolish acres and acres of the most beautiful squares in London.

Yet on that August day of 1946, London, if sadly in need of a coat of paint, still stood. What Hitler's bombers had failed to do had not yet been accomplished by its own citizens.

The Ritz bar was crowded. It was just after six in the evening and its clientele was still mostly military. I looked round but could see no familiar faces, so I pushed my way to the bar and ordered a large Scotch. Looking behind the bar and catching sight of myself in the mirror, I could not help reflecting once again how much I had changed. I determined next day to pay a call on a chemist and see if there was some kind of magical ointment or powder that would take the fierceness out of the red blotches on my face, which had so rightly earned me the name of Captain Blossom. But I did not feel sad or sorry for myself. This, after all, was my first evening of freedom; this is what I had dreamt of for so many years.

After I had drunk my second whiskey, civilian life was even more agreeable, although I would dearly have loved to have someone to talk to.

My hopes were roused when I saw a familiar face come into the bar. It was Guy Burgess. He seemed rather the worse for drink and was leaning for support on a blond young man.

I edged along the bar towards them and said, "Hullo, Guy."

"Who the fucking hell are you?"

This seemed to me inappropriate language for the Ritz bar. But there seemed no point in taking offence so I replied, "Michael Nelson."

"Never fucking heard of you," he replied, and turned his back on me.

This was the last time I saw Guy Burgess. But when he defected to the Russians a few years later I was not at all surprised. In 1939 and 1940, I had met him on several occasions through mutual friends. He seemed to me in those days to be mad. He liked nobody but himself. His political views were dictatorial in the extreme, and I thought at the time that he saw himself as a potential leader of either the Left or the Right. He drank heavily, and how he was permitted to have access to any confidential information in the Foreign Office is beyond my comprehension. Unless of course he was used as a stooge and fed only the information which our Security wanted passed to the other side.

I remember one night in particular when I went to a party of his in Chester Square. He was drinking red wine by the bottle when he became involved in an argument with a blond boy. For Burgess preferred blonds. Suddenly he started screaming at the top of his voice, and before anyone could restrain him he had split open the wretched boy's skull with a bottle. It took about six men to hold him down. Naturally, I was not one of them.

Not having liked Burgess, I was not greatly put out by this refusal to acknowledge me, but drank my drink and wandered along the foyer of the hotel. The Palm Court had not altered one bit. It had always needed a coat of paint ever since I had known it, so it looked as beautiful as ever.

After I had inspected the Palm Court, I made my way to Reception and asked for a room for the night.

"I regret that we are completely full up, Sir."

With that delicacy which I have just explained, a one pound note found its way into the hand of the receptionist, only to be returned with a finesse that exceeded my own.

"I am so sorry not to be able to help you, Sir, but we are absolutely full up."

It was from that moment I fell in love with the Ritz Hotel. Only the receptionist at such a hotel would have declined my offering.

Many would have palmed it, made some pretence of trying to find a room sometime later, knowing perfectly well that there was no hope at all.

"Have you any idea where I could try?" I asked.

"Are you a stranger to London, Sir?"

"Yes. My first night home; my first night in Civvy Street."

"My very good wishes to you, Sir. I am afraid that the hotel accommodation situation in London is chronic, absolutely terrible. At this time of night you will have the greatest difficulty in finding anything of any standard."

"You mean it's the doss-house for me?"

"Not exactly, Sir. Shall I say more of the station kind of accommodation. And you *might* find something in Bloomsbury, but I fear not exactly what you will be seeking."

I was once again about to effect a small transaction by way of thanks, but was prevented from making such a gaffe when the receptionist kept his hands firmly to his sides and said, "I hope we shall have the pleasure of seeing you again, Sir. And once again, may I wish you the best of luck."

Having deposited the cardboard box containing my civilian clothes with the hall porter, I made my way out into the warm air. Piccadilly was crowded, but I determined before I had a further look round, to try and find somewhere to stay for the night. It hardly seemed appropriate that on my first night home I should have to doss down in the park or on the embankment. Besides, there was the question of the English rose I had been promising myself. As if in answer to my thoughts, someone touched my arm and a voice said, "Want a good time, Captain?"

Almost before I could answer, and certainly before I had time to study the form, she had left my side and was accosting two Americans who were loitering under the arches outside the Ritz. I was about to cross the road to catch a bus going towards Bloomsbury when I was accosted a second time. On this occasion I had the good sense to ask, "How much?"

"Two pounds for a short time."

Once again as I did not accept her terms on the spot without haggling, the girl turned away from me and accosted a party of Negro soldiers.

I quickly sensed that I was in a seller's market, and that a speedy decision was essential. But determined to put aside all thoughts of love, sex and lust until I had found a billet, I crossed the road and boarded a bus, but not before I had been accosted a further three times.

It was growing dark as I got off the bus in Bloomsbury and started to make my rounds of the sleazy hotels for which the area was notorious. It was still extremely cheap. Bed and breakfast for five shillings a night and, if the condition of the room was particularly sordid, even less.

After trying a dozen places, and more or less being laughed off the premises for my effrontery in daring to ask for a room so late at night, I began to feel somewhat dispirited, and went into the nearest pub.

At least, although the saloon bar was crowded, there seemed no shortage of beer which was flowing. It was very good beer, too, and cost about a shilling a pint. After I had drunk my second pint I leant across the bar and asked the barmaid if she knew of any place in the area where I might be able to find a room for the night.

"Anyone here know where this gent can put up for the night?" she asked the bar in general.

"It's difficult, ducks," she said to me. "Would put you up myself but my young lad's on leave this week, and he's sleeping on the sofa. Bloody the way they go calling them up if you ask me. The bloody war's over, isn't it? And he's only eighteen, poor boy."

"What's he in?" I asked by way of making conversation.

"The Service Corps."

"That's my mob," I said. "Matter of fact, got home today. Got demobbed into the bargain. Would you like a drink?"

"Don't mind if I do. May I have a gin?"

"Have what you like. You seem all right for booze here."

She winked at me. "The Governor's a right one. Knows where to find the stuff. Never see him here hardly. Always on the go, getting his hands on it."

She turned to the company in general. "Come on, one of you buggers. This officer got home today and out of the bloody army into the bargain. Surely one of you buggers knows where he can doss down for the night."

A middle-aged lady came up to the bar and said, "Look, my brother is the night porter at the Gladstone round the corner. Tell him Gladys sent you, Guvner, and if there's a bed in the place he'll fix it for you. But don't be expecting much. Bit of a rough dive and plenty of coming and going through the night if you get my meaning."

"Would you like a drink?"

"No, that's all right, ducks, pleased to help a gentleman."

I thanked all concerned and, warmed by the whiskey, beer, and having been called a gentleman, I made my way out into the night and found the Gladstone Hotel.

I pushed open the door and walked into a small hall dimly lit by a bulb hanging from the ceiling. It smelt revolting, a mixture of the back streets of Cairo well laced with the effluvia from one of the less expensive brothels of Baghdad. For a moment my courage deserted me, and I was about to turn tail and beat tactical retreat, when a voice said, "What do you want?"

A small, grimey-looking individual, coatless and wearing braces emerged from what once must have been an office. "What do you want?" he repeated as he tottered towards me, and I could see at a glance that he was considerably the worse for drink.

"I want a room, please."

The gentleman in question seemed to find my request extremely humorous, for he burst into uncontrollable laughter interspersed with an ominous wheezing that emerged from his chest and gave the impression that he could not have much longer to live. When he had recovered, he peered up at me and said, "So you want a room?"

This question proved too much, and the performance was repeated, only this time he was left in such a state of exhaustion that he had to retreat into his office where he sat down on a rickety camp bed.

"Gladys sent me," I said, hoping that the word "Gladys" would act as an open sesame.

"Silly cow. Bitch," said my new friend. "I suppose she's on the piss as usual. Didn't think to send me one round, did she?"

"Not actually, but I would be delighted to contribute," I said. I produced a pound note. There was no question of delicacy. Scarcely had I removed the note from my pocket, than he had pounced on it, grabbed it from my grasp and pushed it down the front of his vest.

"So you want a room?" The touch of the real stuff had clearly taken the humour out of the situation.

"Yes, Mr ...?" I decided that politeness and deference were essential. I had nothing to lose but my pride, and clearly I was playing for high stakes with a single room in a doss-house at a premium.

"Call me Fred." He peered up at me. "Officer, aren't you?"

"I'm afraid so." I had no shame at selling my commission short.

"Some Officers is better than others. Had it easy this war, didn't you? Now, our war was different. Real soldiers we was, real soldiers, none of you namby pambies. Gassed I was. Three times. Was you ever gassed?"

"No, Fred. I didn't have that misfortune."

"It's five shillings a night," Fred announced after a pause.

"What is?"

"A room is. Five shillings a night payable in advance."

As I had already parted with a pound, a further advance of five shillings to secure a room seemed a small amount to hazard.

When I had handed over two half-crowns, Fred said, "You've got to sign in, you know." He gave me a wink. "This is a respectable house, Captain, oh yes, a very respectable house." The thought of the Gladstone being a house of virtue once again proved too much for Fred, who proceeded to wheeze and laugh at the same time, so much so that I was sure he was getting in dangerously close contact with his Maker.

Finally, he pulled a tattered hotel register from under his bed and threw it at me.

"Where shall I sign?"

"Where you bloody well like, Captain. You can put your Monica on my arse, for all I care."

I opened the book and read some of the obscenities that had been inscribed in it. The residents of the Hotel Gladstone numbered the cream of the aristocracy. Lord Arseholes of Shitham Hall, Lord and Lady Cunthooks of Anus Castle, to mention just a few, had enjoyed the hospitality of the Gladstone. I noticed too that the President of the United States who gave his address as the White House had been a frequent visitor, and General Eisenhower had graced the premises on several occasions.

Not to be outdone, I wrote Captain Blossom, Ally Slopers Cavalry, The War Office, London. It was the best I could manage at the end of a tiring day.

"I'll show you your room, Captain," said Fred. He took a key from the wall and shuffled across the hall towards the stairs, where he paused and turned.

"Have to take it easy up these stairs, Captain. Gassed, you know. Now that was a real war, not one like you sissies buggered about in. You should have seen the rats. As big as bloody cats they were, as big as bloody cats."

"Don't trouble to come up. Here, give me the key."

Fred drew back, as if I were about to strike him. "Give you the key! What the bloody hell are you thinking of? This is the only bloody key left. It fits all the rooms, and if I lost this bugger I'd be properly fucked up, wouldn't I?"

"I suppose you would be," I was forced to agree.

At the top of the first flight of stairs Fred turned to the left and shuffled along a corridor liberally scattered with empty cartons, tins and other unmentionable objects, until he reached a door at the far end. He stared at it for a minute debating whether it was the right one, muttering to himself all the time. Finally he inserted the key, turned it and swung open the door.

"The bridal suite for the Captain," he announced. Finding this of the greatest humour he proceeded to indulge in another fit of wheezing.

I pushed past him into the room, and switched on the light. A bulb suspended from the ceiling lit up the scene. Obviously lampshades were considered an item of luxury in the Gladstone Hotel.

The room was carpetless and bare except for an iron bedstead covered with a blanket, grey by nature or dirt, I was not able to determine immediately. There was a chair with three legs and an old-fashioned washstand in one corner on which stood a basin and a pitcher.

"How charming. I like it, Fred," I said. "I like it very much."

"We call this one the haunted room," said Fred. "So if you hear noises in the night don't take no notice."

"Haunted?"

"That's what I said." He shuffled across the room and pointed under the bed. "They say you can still see it down there."

"See what?"

"Blood. Bled to death on that bed she did, the poor girl."

"I can see I'm in for a lovely night," I said. "What happened?"

"Big buck he was. Remember him well, a right evil-looking bastard. Brings this young tart back, and that's all there was to it. Cuts her throat from ear to ear. Silly little bitch, should have more sense than to have gone with a nigger just down from the trees."

"Did they catch him?"

"Course they bloody caught him. Strung him up on the gallows they did. Heard he had a neck like a bloody bull. They couldn't break it and a dozen or more had to pull him by the feet before it would give way."

For the first time I noticed the spy hole cut in the door, reminding me of a prison cell.

"I see we're under observation," I remarked.

"The proprietor of this knocking shop didn't want no more trouble," said Fred, "so he had these spy holes cut. Now don't you worry, Captain. If you want to bring a bit of what you fancy back, all you've got to do is to hang your trousers on the back of the door and no one will be able to watch you on the job. Funny thing that, never did fancy watching other blokes at it, but I get a number of people coming to me and offering me money to go round peering through these peepholes. Some of them are ladies too, all la-ti-da and posh. You'd have thought they'd seen enough cock in their lives without having to pay to see other people's. Well, I better be getting back to my office, Captain. Don't forget to lock the door on the inside when you go to bed or some bugger will nick everything, and that's for sure. Had a Major in the other night. Silly sod goes to sleep with this tart and when they woke up in the morning all their clothes had gone, leaving them both as the day they were born. Right laugh it was. Had the devil of a job fixing them up so that they could leave respectable like. Cost them a bomb it did, too. Had to buy the stuff all on the Black Market. Can't even get a shirt without bloody coupons these days, Captain. Sometimes I wake up and think we must have lost the fucking war."

Looking round the room which was to harbour me on my first night back in the Old Country as a civilian, I was inclined to agree with Fred.

I accompanied him downstairs, where his last words to me were, "When you come in, Captain, don't forget to lock your door. And if you bring a bit back with you, watch your fucking wallet like a hawk. The girls aren't what they used to be, I can tell you. No giving value for money these days. Nothing but a load of fucking whores on the make."

The air of Southampton Row was sweet compared with that inside the Gladstone. It was now after eleven o'clock and the streets were becoming more crowded as the public houses were beginning to close. I considered the idea of going to a night-club, possibly to my old haunt the Embassy in Bond Street. On the other hand, I was beginning to feel tired, which was not surprising since it was less than forty-eight hours since I had left Naples, and my induction into Civvy Street had not been without adventures.

As I approached Tottenham Court Road, I became conscious of

the vast hordes of prostitutes operating on all sides. They were as numerous as they had been in the streets of Naples and Rome in the early days of the Allied Occupation of Italy, where the going rate for a girl from a high class family had been a tin of bully, and for a scrubber off the streets, a couple of cigarettes.

The proximity of this sex market brought me once again to thoughts of love, even if that is not the right word. I should have said thoughts of lust. But the competition was fast and furious. There was no opportunity to promenade slowly while one made up one's mind. Bargains were being struck on all sides with the speed of lightning. I noticed that members of the American forces wasted no time, nor did the girls ever seem to object to the terms offered. On the other hand the English soldiers hung about in a dejected state and I realized that they were feeling extremely bitter at being outbid by their allies from across the Atlantic.

Having decided that this was no place for me, I decided to return to the Gladstone, and try to get some sleep.

Seldom in my life has fortune smiled on me. And as I retraced my steps in the direction of the Gladstone, I could not help reflecting that my friend, John Fish, would never have found himself in my situation on his first night as a civilian. I could picture him as I walked slowly back down the Tottenham Court Road, giving a party in one of the best hotels in London, surrounded on all sides by adoring females.

I was about to enter the Gladstone when a voice behind me said, "Are you looking for anything?"

I turned, expecting to see yet another scrubber ogling me from the shadows. To begin with I could only make out a slight and small figure, but as she stepped closer to me, I saw that she was a young girl. She could not have been more than seventeen.

"Are you looking for anything?" she repeated diffidently.

"I'm looking for someone like you," I said.

"It will cost you two pounds," she said, and I detected a slight Scottish burr in her accent.

I took her by the arm. "What's your name?"

"Margaret," she said.

"Well, I'm afraid I can't exactly offer you the hospitality of the Ritz," I said, "but I should be delighted to entertain you at the Gladstone."

"Two pounds," she said.

I took two pounds out of my pocket and gave them to her. She opened her bag and put the money inside.

When we had reached my room, remembering Fred's advice I locked the door, took off my battle dress top and hung it from a hook in the door so that it covered the spy hole.

Margaret sat down on the edge of the bed and removed her blouse. I could not help noticing how shy she was, and it occurred to me that she must be very new to the game.

"How long have you been doing this?" I asked.

"None of your business."

She removed her skirt, crossed to the basin, took off her pants and washed herself. I found the action so mechanical, that I was reminded of an animal being led to the slaughter.

She was still wearing her bra, when she went to the bed and lay down on it.

"Come on, what are you waiting for?" she said.

I went to the bed, still dressed, and stood looking down at her.

"What are you staring at?" she asked. And, as if she were embarrassed, she placed her hands across her bra as if to shield her breasts from my gaze.

"Are you one of those that likes to talk?" she suddenly said. "Is it your wife who doesn't understand you? It'll cost you more if you want anything kinky. Or do you just want to talk dirty. If that's what you want, I can talk ever so dirty, but it'll cost you another pound."

"No I don't want to talk dirty," I said. "And I don't want to play kinky, not tonight anyway."

"That's something to be thankful for. Come on then, don't stand there like a loon. Get on and fuck me."

I went to the basin and emptied the water from the basin which she had used, refilled it and washed myself.

"You don't say much," she called out. "Don't you fancy me? Or are you one of those who can't get a hard on?"

I turned towards her.

"Not bad," she said. "Come on then, let's get it over with."

I walked towards the bed. She opened her legs and pointed a finger between them. Presumably to keep me excited she said "You're going to fuck my pussy, aren't you?"

"Yes."

"You are a strange one. Can't you speak or something?" Suddenly she sat up and said, "You haven't got a rubber on. No one fucks me without a rubber, not even the King of England."

The thought of the King of England fucking in the Gladstone Hotel made me laugh aloud.

"What's so funny? Come on, a rubber or no fuck. I'll just have to rub you off."

I went back to the chair where I had thrown my trousers, and felt down in the pocket specially built for French letters, and came up with a blue packet marked *"Por il climate tropicale."* They were a consignment that had been captured from the Italians in the desert.

When I had prepared myself, I returned to the bed and laid down beside her.

"Here, none of that," she said. "You can't expect me to stay here all night for a couple of quid."

She put her fingers in her mouth, moistened them with her spittle, and rubbed them across the French letter.

"That'll help you in."

That's true love, I thought to myself. I clambered on top of her about as gracefully as a bull in a pen.

She made no pretence of enjoyment, and I could feel her mind was far away. And that was the best place it could be. I would say here that, while I have never disapproved of prostitution from the woman's point of view, I have always thought it second best from the customer's. If anyone is harmed it is the latter.

"What are you mumbling about?" she complained. "Come on, I haven't got all night." And in an attempt to bring me to a quick climax, she whispered in what she imagined to be a sexy voice, "Come on soldier, fuck me hard, soldier."

When I had finished and rolled off her, she asked, "What was all that nonsense you were talking about? What's all that about an English rose?"

# 3

When I came downstairs the following morning Fred shambled out of his office looking worried.

"Are you all right, Captain? You haven't lost anything?"

"Only another illusion," I said.

"Right tart that one is. Very light on the fingers."

I felt in my pockets, checked my money, but nothing seemed to be missing.

"Sets some poor sods up too, she does," said Fred. "Gets some poor old bugger on the job and then in rush a couple of toughs who rough the poor fellow up for messing about with their sister. Sister my arse. Don't like to see that kind of thing going on. This is a respectable house, this is, Captain. I mean, within reason."

I said good-bye to Fred, shook him by the hand, and promised him that I would be back. Then I went round the corner to have a drink, collect my wits, and make plans for the immediate future.

Fairly soon I would have to establish contact with my family. In practical terms this meant going to see my father. My mother had died the previous year, while I had still been in Italy, and my father had moved from the large house at Ascot where my family had lived before the war to a house near Newbury. Since my mother's death he had married again.

I decided, however, that I would first go to Ascot. This was in no way due to any desire to indulge in nostalgia. It was simply that the first person I wanted to see on my return to Civvy Street was Bill Jarman.

Bill Jarman had been my father's batman when he had served in the gunners during the 1914–18 war. Early on in that war my father had been wounded but he had never lost touch with Bill. Certainly Bill had been at my father's wedding in 1917. One of Bill's favourite stories was how he had noticed some specks of dust on my father's field boots just as my father was about to leave for the church. He had dashed forward to wipe them clean. Putting his hand in his pocket he had taken out what he imagined to be a duster. The duster had been a pair of lady's knickers.

After the war Bill had worked in a steel works in Bristol. He had been injured in an accident. In the late twenties he found himself unemployed.

One day he arrived at our house at Ascot. My father had taken him on as a general factotum and assistant gardener.

Bill stayed with us until the second war broke out and our family disintegrated. But during all those years he had become more of a father to me than my own father. The truth of the matter was that I was frightened of my own father, and Bill made an admirable substitute. I poured out all my troubles to him, confided all my ambitions in him, and trusted him completely. When I hopped it from my prep school in the early thirties, I did not run to my father, but to Bill.

When Bill first came to Ascot he had lived in a cottage about a mile and a half from the house. But after a disagreement between my father and the head gardener who had departed, Bill had moved into the rooms which he vacated over the garage together with his wife and two children. Here I had often gone when I was young to pour out my troubles over numerous cups of sweet tea. And as I had grown older many were the hours I had spent there in political discussions with Bill. In the late thirties I was politically to the extreme Left, while Bill was a more moderate supporter of the Labour party. Much as I disagreed with my father, and critical as I may be of him today even though he is dead, I greatly admire him for respecting Bill's political opinions although he himself was a staunch Tory. I think that I afforded him considerable pleasure in the last years of his life by gradually moving away from the Left to Center, and then to the Right. He always used to say to me that no man has a heart if he is not a socialist before he is twenty-one and that he is a damned fool if he is still one at twenty-two.

It was about one o'clock that the train from Waterloo reached Ascot. I walked across the racecourse and turned into the drive. The first thing I noticed was that the gate was badly in need of a touch of paint. During my first week back in England it was this lack of paint, the universal drabness, that struck me more than anything else. But after seven days I accepted it, and ceased to notice or care.

I walked down the drive and circled the house. The house itself had changed little, but I was shocked at the state of the garden. It ran in all to nine acres, and everywhere there were signs of neglect. The lawns were unmown, the rose beds had disappeared under a mass of weeds, and the herbaceous borders were a jungle.

I knew the house had been occupied by evacuees during the war, but it had never occurred to me that they would have allowed the grounds to deteriorate so completely.

I went in through the front door. It was as if I was back in barracks. There were no carpets on the floor, just bare boards everywhere and extremely dirty ones at that.

I stood in the hall and looked round. There was desolation and destruction on all sides. The bannisters had been torn down in several places, the panelling had been ripped from the walls exposing areas of plaster. Numerous panes were missing from the windows. There was a smell of damp about the place together with the stink of unwashed bodies and human excreta. I might just have well been back in Italy looking for billets for my men in any one of the thousands of ruined villages.

Strangely enough I was not shocked. I stood there for several minutes more amazed than anything else. How could this have happened? The place had not been bombed; it had not been occupied by a hostile power.

"What do you want?"

I turned and saw that a woman had come out from the door that led off the hall into what had been the drawing room.

When I did not reply she came up to me and repeated: "What's your business?"

She spoke with a Cockney accent. She was wearing a pair of men's trousers and a red shirt, over which she had draped a battle dress blouse. From the corner of her lips drooped a cigarette.

"I used to live here," I said.

"I bet you don't recognize the old place now," she said. "They tell me it was right posh before the war."

"I never heard that," I said. "I just lived here. It was my home."

"Plenty of servants and all that jazz they tell me. Three in the garden and six in the house, weren't there?"

"Something like that," I said, thinking how odd it was to hear someone speak of the people with whom I had grown up in terms of numbers rather than as human beings.

"Can you tell me if Bill Jarman is still at the cottage?"

"No, crowd of bloody Jews over there. Filthy people too. You don't want to go near that lot."

"Do you know where he lives?"

"He's down at South Ascot, somewhere near the pub. Used to come up here regular until a few years ago and mess about in the kitchen garden. Then one day he said he couldn't stand it any longer and we've not seen him since."

"How long have you been here?" I asked.

"Too bloody long. Since the Blitz when we was evacuated down here. It must have been your old man who was still living here. Posh geezer with a tash."

I smiled at this description of my father. Posh he never was, except when he used to go to the City and that had been many years ago. His clothes used usually to consist of a pair of ill-fitting corduroys and an ancient tweed jacket.

"Yes, too bloody long," she continued. "Can't wait to get back to the smoke and a bit of civilization. Trouble is there are no bloody houses. Jerry knocked them down, and we've put this lot in power to build new ones for us, but nothing seems to happen."

"Don't you like it here?"

"How can we like it? No one to talk to, nothing to do, the nearest boozer two miles away and then no bloody beer when we get there. Kids running wild and fighting with the locals. It's no place for people like us. The sooner we get back where we belong the happier we shall be."

"Are there many of you left here?" I asked. The war had been over for more than a year and it had come as a surprise to me to find our house still being occupied by evacuees. I remember something my father had written about it in a letter to me while I had still been in Italy. He had complained bitterly that the Socialist Government was refusing to move the evacuees into centralized accommodation, with the result that thousands of houses were only partially occupied so that they could not be sold on the open market with vacant possession, or returned to their owners.

"No, most of them have gone," she said. "Just the nine of us in the main house, six or seven in the Children's Wing, and then there's the Jews in the cottage."

I was amused to hear her refer to one part of the house as the Children's Wing, and wondered how the name had stuck. It had been built on to the house in the early thirties when my father had decided that the house should be split down the middle segregating the children from the grown-ups. This practice may seem odd today, but was quite usual in those times. I suppose when the evacuee families had been allocated accommodation in the house while my father was still in residence, he must have still talked about the Children's Wing, and so the name had passed into common use.

"It must be odd for someone like you coming back and seeing the old place in a state like this," she said.

"I suppose it is," I said. "I'd never thought about it until this moment."

"You'll find a lot has changed," she said. "Been away long?"

"Four years overseas."

"Then you're in for a shock or two. We've a Labour Government in power now, and it's all going to be different." She paused. "Don't get me wrong. I'm not against any one. It's just the old system I hated. You know, THEM and US. That's all got to go. It's to be fair's fair for all from now on, and each one as good as the other. And there's the welfare state. Do you know what that Beveridge said on the radio the other night? He said he's going to look after us from the cradle to the grave."

I was encouraged to hear the enthusiasm in her voice. Perhaps my years in the army had not been wasted. The men who had fought in the First World War had struggled to make the world safe for democracy. Their cup of bitterness had run over when they saw that all they had produced was Fascism, Communism, and a Second World War. I would die happily in the knowledge that I had made life from the cradle to the grave more secure.

I was about to go up the stairs to have a look around, when something told me not to. You can call it premonition. More likely it was common sense on my part. Instead I said good-bye to my companion who looked at me oddly and said: "You're a funny one. Don't seem to be a bit upset do you?"

"It wouldn't do any good, would it?" I said.

It wasn't until I reached the gate that it dawned on me that something important had happened to me. It was something that I had known for the last five and a half years, ever since the day I had gone into the army. I would never return to live in the house at Ascot. My life there belonged to the past and my life was never going to be the same as it had been in the twenties and thirties.

This obvious conclusion did not make me the slightest bit sad. It did not induce in me a nostalgic longing for the past. It was a simple fact that I could not avoid. As I walked out of the gate that badly needed a coat of paint, I knew it was for the last time.

As a matter of fact that is not true. Two years ago I happened to be passing the house and I drove down the drive. I stopped by the front door and got out of the car. To my delight and amazement the house had returned to exactly as it had looked in my childhood and adolescence. The roses were in full bloom on the walls, the tennis courts were carefully mown. I wandered through the rose garden and on all sides there was a sweet scent. The statue in the middle of the pool, whom we had all known as Fanny but no doubt bore some more worthy classical name, still stood holding her shell upwards, although minus one arm; the herbaceous borders were back to their former glory. There were changes of course. Where there had once been a kitchen garden there now stood two brand new bungalows. Most surprising of all, in the orchard there was not the slightest trace of the swimming pool. It seemed odd that a hole in the ground could disappear so completely. I was coming back from the orchard when a charming lady stopped me and asked if she could help me. I told her who I was and she was most helpful and informed me that the house now belonged to a housing association and had been divided into five or six flats and that they all contributed to the upkeep of the garden. She invited me into the house, but I declined her offer. The day I had gone there one year after the war to find Bill Jarman I was not susceptible to nostalgia.

Half an hour later I was knocking on Bill Jarman's door in South Ascot.

Bill let out a shout, took my hand, and pumped it up and down. That's something I shall always remember about Bill. He was always pleased to see me whenever I called on him and at whatever hour. He turned and shouted: "Mum it's Mick."

Mrs Jarman came running to the door and I flung my arms around her and kissed her.

"Goodness me, you haven't half put some weight on, Mick," she said.

"Nonsense, Ma," said Bill. "It's just all that army grub he's been noshing."

"I'll put the pot on right away," she said.

"Mick would like something a bit stronger I expect," said Bill. "Afraid there's nothing in the house, Mick, but we could slip down to the pub and see if they've got anything."

"Tea would do me fine," I said. I had already noticed that Mrs

Jarman had gone to the china cabinet and was getting out her best cups and saucers. I had always teased her about these and told her that they were reserved for funerals and marriages.

While Mrs Jarman was getting the tea, Bill and I went into the front room and sat down.

"Off you go, Mick. Tell me your news."

I never hid anything from Bill. So I proceeded to tell him about my last year of Italy, about my dealings in the Black Market, about my love life, about my brush with the Mafia, and my narrow escape from a Court Martial only forty-eight hours previously.

"You won't find things much different over here, Mick," said Bill. "The whole country's on the fiddle from one end to the other. You're bound to get it when everything's in short supply. There's a Black Market in everything you care to think of."

"We do all right," said Mrs Jarman. "Bill's the biggest scrounger of the lot. He makes rings round them all."

I knew that Mrs Jarman was speaking the truth. Bill was a real old soldier, a master at "borrowing". If there was one thing that soldiers of all ages and of all countries have in common, it is the art of scrounging.

"Now, now, Ma, you're not complaining are you? How would you like to have to live on our ration books?"

"You couldn't do it," she said. "I don't suppose you know what they expect us to live on, Mick, seeing as you've been overseas so long. Two ounces of butter a week, a shilling's worth of meat, one rasher of bacon and one egg, and a couple of ounces of tea. And there's the points. So many points for this and so many for that. But the daft thing is it's all rubbish anyway. What about that snook or whatever you call it."

"Tinned dogfish," said Bill.

"Whatever it was, the cat brought it up," she said.

Bill told me that he was now working at the Telephone Exchange. He hoped soon to be promoted to the post of Supervisor and would eventually retire with a good pension.

"Of course that's all very nice, Mick," he said. "In fact it's great to be living with a Labour Government in power though I daresay it's driving your old man up the pole. But I always told him it was bound to come. It stood to reason didn't it that as soon as the masses saw which side their bread was buttered they would vote their own people into power."

"Mick doesn't want to talk politics," said Mrs Jarman.

"Course he does, Ma. Don't you remember all those nights before the war when he used to come to the cottage and tell us how he and the Communist Party were going to put the world to rights?" He paused.

"Don't get me wrong, Mick, they weren't bad days as far as we were concerned. Nor for that matter for anyone who worked for your old man. He was a fair guvner. And your mother in the house, now she was a real lady. Do you know, Mick, there isn't a person in the village who would say a hard word about her. She was a saint. Did a lot more for people who needed help than any of you knew. Everyone misses her. What a tragedy."

"It's a pity she and your old man split up," said Mrs Jarman.

"It's just one of those things," said Bill. "I told your old man I thought he was in the wrong and he knows that I meant it."

"It was a shame, a terrible shame," said Mrs Jarman.

It is very difficult to know what happens between two people when their marriage breaks up. My mother had been ill when my father had left her for someone else whom he subsequently married. I loved my mother very much. I do not think that I ever loved my father in the same way. He had been too remote. Sometimes I think he never loved his children. Possibly they reminded him of his youth as he grew older. An extraordinary thing about my father is that he always looked old to me. When I was six he looked an old man. He still looked old when I was seventeen. And when I was fifty which was the last time I saw him he still seemed to me exactly the same as he had been when I was six—just old.

I had met my father's wife-to-be during my short leave from Italy in 1945, while I was waiting to go to the Far East. I never went because the atomic bomb had been dropped on Japan. My mother was still alive, but in a nursing home. I had worried a great deal about the situation, but had come to the conclusion that whatever I might say would not make the slightest difference. I could have turned my back on my father, but I would have achieved nothing. In any case my own life had not been blameless, nor was it to be in the future. If at any time I have ever felt bitter about my father I remind myself that without his assistance I could not have lived on this earth. I have been one of the lucky ones; I was born into a rich family in the Western Hemisphere. I have on the whole been granted an easy and pleasurable life.

Naturally Bill and I discussed the days before the war. We talked of my mother and father, my brothers and sisters, and roared with laughter as we recalled what Bill called those "bad old days."

"Yes, Mick, make no mistake, they were hard days for the working classes and the two million unemployed. That's why I welcome this Labour Government. It's going to do great things for the country, believe me."

"He's not telling the truth, Mick," said Mrs Jarman. "Sometimes at night he sits up talking about all of you, and about the fun we all had. Yes, that's the truth, Mick, whatever he says. He can go on spouting about this Labour Government till the cows come home, but he loved those days at Ascot before the war. Come on, you silly old devil, own up and speak the truth."

"I've never denied it, Ma," said Bill. "Those days were not so bad for us, but not for the poor sods on the dole. Yes, it was fun all right. We did have a sense of belonging, and I'll say one thing, there was no sense of class at the house. And everyone was looked after. I wasn't afraid to tell the old man off if I felt he was in the wrong. Mind you, I never tried it before midday. A right bugger he was before midday, I don't mind telling you."

"How is everybody else?" I asked. "I was thinking of the maids who had worked in the house, Bunty, Mary, Audrey, Cook and the others."

"They miss it too," said Mrs Jarman. "They miss your mum most of all."

I did not know what to make of this. I wondered if Mrs Jarman was just being sentimental. I think Bill could sense my doubts, for he said: "That's right, Mick. We all miss it. Whenever we meet we have a natter about the old days and a good laugh. But they'll never come back. You realize that don't you?"

"No, they'll never come back. I realized a few hours ago they would never come back."

Two hours later, after having drunk a couple of pints of bitter with Bill in the local pub, I shook him by the hand and set out for my father's new house near Newbury.

I was most agreeably surprised when I walked up the drive to find that my father had bought a beautiful Queen Anne house. For whatever else my father may have had it was not good taste. It was in fact the most pleasant house he was to live in during the remaining years of his life.

As I have already written, my father had been wounded in the Kaiser's war. He had been peppered by shrapnel in the stomach and leg. As a result of the wound in his stomach he lived in a permanent state of diarrhoea, which must have made life very unpleasant for him. So that when I write anything derogatory about him I have to remind myself that he was very often in a state of great discomfort.

The shrapnel in his leg afforded me considerable amusement. It was one of his party tricks to roll up his trousers and display the pieces which could be seen and felt below the skin, to any admiring female that happened to be handy. Sometimes these pieces of shrapnel would work their way to the surface, then he would have to go into hospital to have them removed. When I was about seven years old he had several lumps removed in Windsor Hospital. He gave them to me and I kept them in a bottle. Unfortunately, like all my other possessions they were lost in my absence during the war.

My father was a fine handyman and a keen gardener. Unfortunately houses were his downfall. He would work like a slave getting the place in order. He would be up at first light laying out new beds, terraces, lawns and herbaceous borders. Even before the war when he had employed three gardeners at Ascot, he had always worked alongside them when he could find the time. Afterwards he had no one to help him, not because he could not afford to employ anybody, although like many people of his class he saw himself ruined and a poor man, but because no one in the new social climate would have dreamt of taking up gardening as a career. There were a few old hands about, identifiable by their collarless shirts held together at the front by one stud, but they were few and in constant demand. The extraordinary thing is that they were still remarkably cheap to employ in relation to post-war rates of pay. The upper and middle-classes always know a good thing when they see one, and they did not consider in their interests, let alone their duty, to increase the wages of these retainers. In fact, had anyone done so, they would have been considered traitors, the kind of people who did not play the game. Gradually however these old-fashioned workers grew wise to the fact that they were being exploited. According to my father, they were corrupted by the war profiteers to whom money meant nothing and who bid far too much for their services.

I have said that houses were my father's downfall. After months and months of hard work, he would get the house and the garden exactly to his liking. On occasions this might include the construction of a vast rockery whose stones weighing hundredweights he would ease into position without any outside assistance. The summer would come, the flowers would bloom, and he would mow the lawns and keep the edges trim. From dawn to dusk he would be in the garden, and his friends would come and say how wonderful he was and that he was blessed with green fingers.

Then would come the crunch. One day he would wake up racked with aches and pains and announce that it was "too much." The house would be put on the market and the search would be set in motion for something more manageable. As he would remark to his friends, he wasn't as young as he used to be and the time had come for him to ease up.

Finally he would move into a new house. It would be remarkable for two things. It would be larger than the one he had just vacated, and inevitably the garden would be in a state of neglect. At vast expense, he would buy new carpets and fit them himself. Extra cupboard space was invariably called for, and sometimes the kitchen would have to be enlarged, which necessitated the demolition of a wall or two. All these alterations he would carry out himself, working from first light to last.

Next the garden would have to be brought under control. This might take a year or two.

When all was shipshape and Bristol fashion, he would announce that once again it was all "too much." The house would be put on the market. ...

On one occasion he really did try to retrench. He bought a small semi-detached house in Hungerford High Street. With it went commoners rights which entitled him to free fishing on the River Kennet and I believe that had he been so inclined he could have shot at the duck on the marshes at the time of the year when it is legal to kill duck with a gun.

To my knowledge he only spent a few nights in that particular house. He did not even wait to lick it into shape before moving on. He announced that he could on no account live in a hen coop, it gave him claustrophobia. So almost before he and his wife were in, they were on their way to something with an even larger garden and more rooms than the house they had sold before moving into the semi-detached.

Although my father was in one of his depressed moods I think he was genuinely pleased to see me. He was sitting on the lawn with his new wife Jane when I arrived, and quickly disappeared into the house, to emerge a few minutes later carrying a bottle of champagne immersed in a bucket of ice.

"He's kept this specially for your home-coming," she said.

"The last of the old cellar," my father sighed. "Can't afford to keep decent wine these days even if I could lay my hands on the stuff. Do you know what I used to pay before the war for that Hock we used to drink every night at dinner? Twenty shillings a dozen. A lovely wine it was too."

I had to agree. If there was one thing he was never mean about, it was drink. There had always been plenty of drink at Ascot, sherry before lunch, and beer or cider with it. Cocktails at six and wine every night at dinner, with port at the end. Then in case one should be thirsty during the night, at half-past ten a tray on which were Whitbread beer and whiskey was brought into the drawing room by one of the maids, and everybody would help himself.

I cannot recall much about the first evening with my father and Jane, except that the former spent most of the evening complaining about the changes that had taken place in the country, all for the worst. Even the fishing on the Kennet was now hardly worth troubling about. The stock of trout had been allowed to run down, they had gone backwards rather than forwards (in weight), and the water was infested with damned grayling. Personally I had a partiality for grayling. Not only did I enjoy fishing for them with a fly on a bright autumn day, I preferred their flavour to that of trout.

But I do remember that a few of their friends came for drinks before dinner. This I gathered was an event, because drink was hard to come by. It could only be procured at vast expense on the Black Market, and this was not always easy because the sources of supply were constantly shifting. I gathered that whereas a certain person or store might have a supply of gin or whiskey that was kept behind the counter one week, the next week it might be necessary to bicycle several miles to obtain a further supply. The car was used in emergencies only.

"Can't you get petrol on the Black Market?" I asked.

"Of course, but there's no point in wasting money. You don't actually buy petrol. You buy the coupons. The going rate per coupon is five shillings which is more than the petrol costs," my father informed me.

Because I was so steeped in shady practices during my last year in Italy, it did not strike me at all odd that someone like my father, who before the war had been a pillar of society, had sat on the local bench as a Justice of the Peace, should have joined the ranks of the scroungers. What is more he had thrown himself whole-heartedly into the business, and was clearly well versed in all departments of shady dealing.

The guests were of two kinds. There were the local gentry and the local tradesmen. I must confess that I found this mixture strange.

The local gentry were well represented by a retired Colonel straight from the pages of Punch, waxed moustache, bellowing voice, purple veins on the face and all. I remember him vividly to this day. He informed me that he had spent the best of his military years of service in Constantinople, which he referred to as Constant. "A great city is Constant, my boy," he whispered to me confidentially, "plenty of hunting, shooting and fishing, and all the other 'ings."

I began to understand why so many of the local tradesmen had been asked to drinks when I overheard a confidential conversation between Jane and the local butcher. I had assumed up to that point that I was witnessing one of the social changes in New Socialist Britain.

"We'll be slaughtering on Saturday, my dear," I heard him whisper. "And I'll be sure you get as lovely a leg of pork that you ever did see in your life."

"Shall I pay you now, Bert?" said Jane reaching for her bag.

"Just as you wish, my dear," said Bert holding out his hand.

Several notes passed hands, but, I regret to say, without that delicacy of touch that I myself had perfected.

In the course of the early part of the evening I was able to watch several shady deals being brought to happy conclusions. But it seemed to my experienced eyes that it was too much of a sellers' market. There was far too little haggling. The buyers, including my father and my step-mother, seemed to have had all the stuffing knocked out of them. I did not approve of seeing the butcher and the garage owner having it all their own way. I took a particular dislike to the owner of the local wine stores. To begin with he was too well dressed, and secondly he was far too pleased with himself.

"Did very well in the war," Jane said to me noticing that I had got my eyes on him.

"You mean he got decorated?" I said incredulously.

"Don't be silly, Mick. Reserved occupation. A bricklayer I believe. Worked on Government contracts, and was able to save enough to buy the wine store."

"Whose owner was in the forces," I added.

"That's right," said Jane. "And jolly well he's done out of it too."

Reminding myself that my own war record was nothing of

which I could be proud, I contented myself with downing as much of the foul cocktail that my father had mixed for his guests. I was to discover that in the immediate post-war years in the country at least, one had to be prepared to drink the most evil-tasting concoctions that man could devise, or go without. If there's one thing I detest it's a cup of any sort and in those years cup really and truly came into its own. The basic object of a cup is to make the drink go as far as possible with the minimum of alcohol and the maximum of non-alcoholic juices. For instance, a typical cup of those days would be a flagon of cider, the skin of one orange if available, a bottle of fizzy lemonade decorated with a sprig of mint and a dandelion.

I was quickly to learn that the true mark of friendship was when you were called to one side, often into a private room, where one would be offered a drop of the real stuff.

After the guests had departed Jane produced an excellent meal. Roast chicken, roast potatoes, fresh peas from the garden, and bread sauce, followed by apple pie and cream. And in case anyone might still feel hungry a piece of cheddar weighing at least two pounds was placed on the table, which considering the ration was about two ounces of cheese per person per week, was generous in the extreme.

Before I retired to bed that night my father suggested that I might care to have a day's fishing on the Kennet the following day, adding that we could not expect to catch anything as the water had been allowed to fall into the hands of a lot of damned fools.

"And we could have a little talk at the same time," he concluded as he bid me good-night at my bedroom door.

I was surprised next day when we drove up Hungerford High Street to see long queues snaking outside several of the shops.

"Bloody fools, they'll queue for anything," said my father. "When they get to the head of the queue they don't even know what they've been waiting for."

"What are they after?" I asked.

"Fruit, things like oranges and bananas. Groceries of all kinds, butter, and meat. You saw what it was about last night, didn't you?"

"Frankly I was a bit shocked. They were such boring people," I said.

"My dear boy, you can't afford to be a snob these days. It's every man for himself."

"I thought we had a socialist government in power."

"Socialist my foot. They're just as bad as the rest of us. All they can think about is feathering their own nests. Mark my words, my boy, this is the end of England. You'll remember me saying this long after I've gone."

"But everyone tells me we've won the war," I said.

"And lost the peace."

We parked the car at the bottom of the town and walked to the bridge. My father leaned over it and sighed: "I remember this water when it was really good and had some large fish in it. Just look at it now. Not a thing moving."

"You should have kept that stretch of water up towards Marlborough," I said.

"I suppose I should have done," he said.

That was another extraordinary thing about my father. He was a rich man, but he never seemed to get value for his money. If he did he lost interest. The stretch of water towards Marlborough had been first class, but like his houses, he always wanted to move on, to change to something new, which always proved disastrous.

At the same time he could be an obstinate man, the kind of person who would never forget, and could become obsessional. There was the case of the outboard motor. He bought it for his children to use on our two dinghies we kept in Devon where we would spend our holidays. I think it only cost about seventeen pounds. During the war my eldest brother kept it at his house. At one time he lent it to a cousin of ours in Scotland. Suddenly after the war my father decided that it was his outboard motor and he wanted it back. He wrote letters to all of us demanding to know its whereabouts. In his eyes it had become a pearl beyond price. It was not even as if he wanted to use it. He hated the sea. Finally in a fury my brother retrieved it from Scotland, put it in a sack, and returned it to my father. It must have been smashed to smithereens when it arrived. But my father never said a word about it. I can only assume that he was satisfied to get back what he regarded as his own property, even if it was only fit for scrap.

Later on, when he and Jane were divorced, he became obsessional about his stamp collection. I do not believe for one moment that it was valuable. But when he married his third wife, this stamp collection caused him sleepness nights. The trouble was that Jane would not return it, and I believe in due course she sold it. If she got a hundred pounds for it, she would have been lucky. But it immediately began to assume a vast value in his eyes. Jane, he would declare to me verbally and in letters, had robbed him of a fortune. Up to the time of his death the imaginary value of this collection continued to haunt him and rise to astronomic sums.

As we leant over Hungerford Bridge, there was no sign of activity from the trout, although a fair amount of fly was going down on the surface.

"I suppose we might as well stroll down the bank before lunch," he said. "But I don't expect anything will be moving."

He was quite right. Either there were no fish in the water, or they had gone off flies. Nevertheless I enjoyed walking with my father. It is a very beautiful river, and I suppose I came closest to my father when I was with him on a fishing expedition, even if we caught no fish.

We were sitting in the fishing hut when he opened the conversation which I knew must come when he had said the previous night that we must have a little talk.

"What are you going to do, my boy?"

"I haven't the faintest idea. Have a look around, find my bearings, and get accustomed to being back in Civvy Street."

"You're going to discover everything is very different from when you went away."

"So everybody is anxious to tell me," I said.

"Haven't you noticed it already?" he asked.

"In a way. But you must realize that at the moment I'm in a state of euphoria. The sheer heaven of getting out of the army is all that I can feel."

"You can't live on euphoria for ever."

"I know. So just let me enjoy it while it's still with me."

"Well, don't drift too long. What about going back to newspapers?"

"It's a possibility," I said. I felt slightly annoyed. "I've only been back three days. Give me a chance."

"You don't want to waste too much time. Things have changed, my boy."

I looked out at the river. Although there was not a sign of a fish moving, the river and the valley looked as beautiful to me as it ever had done. To put an end to our little talk I said: "What about a drink?"

We went back to the bridge and up the High Street to the Feathers, whose landlord was an old friend of my father, and who was happy to serve us with whiskey and gin.

I don't know whether my uncooperative attitude had upset him, but at one o'clock my father announced that both his leg and his guts were playing him up and that he would go home for lunch and leave me to get on with the fishing, adding that he did not believe there was a single decent fish left in the river. I was in two minds as to whether to accompany him, when into the bar walked John Fish.

"What on earth brings you here?" I asked after I had introduced him to my father.

"Happen to be passing. You probably don't remember, but when I saw you during your adventures at Aldershot, you gave me your father's address. As I happened to be passing I decided to drop in just in case you had already deserted the Big City, and Mrs Nelson said you were fishing in Hungerford, so all I had to do was to search the pubs for you."

When my father had bought both of us a drink, and still said that he would go home, I was sure that I had upset him. But before he left the bar he asked John to come in later for a drink at the house if he had nothing better to do.

"So that's your Old Man" said John when we were alone. "Seems a harmless enough chap to me. The way you described him in Italy you made him out a right ogre."

"I can't help being frightened of him," I said. "It's the way I was brought up. He was a God at home, and it's difficult to change the image overnight."

"How you enjoying Civvy Street?"

"Slightly disastrous last night. Not quite what I had hoped for, but at least it was funny."

I related to John the story of my night at the Gladstone Hotel, omitting not a single sordid detail.

At two-thirty we were thrown out of the bar, by which time we had consumed a fair amount of alcohol. John announced that he would like to go for a swim.

It was a very hot afternoon as we drove in John's army staff car in the direction of Marlborough. It seemed strange that here I was a civilian since the previous day, already back with my old army friend driving in a transport belonging to His Majesty. It was as if the tentacles of the army were reaching out after me, determined that I should not escape.

About five miles out of Hungerford John turned off the main road and we bumped down a narrow track, which ended at a ford. I could hardly stop laughing when John went to the tool box of the car, and came back carrying a bottle of Scotch and two glasses. A few minutes later we had stripped down to our pants, and were sitting in the rapids sipping whiskey.

Soon I began to feel slightly drunk, and stretched out full length letting the water wash over me, as I gazed through the trees at the blue sky beyond.

"This is what I'd like to do in Civvy Street," I announced. "Lie here for ever and ever sipping Scotch and feeling the cold water between my toes."

"You're pissed," said John. "In fact, Michael, I've very worried about you. What are you going to do?"

"Not you too! The Old Man has already been getting at me."

"But you're totally inadequate," said John. "There is nothing you can do."

"Except lie here and sip whiskey," I said. "Gather ye rosebuds while ye may, old time is still a flying."

John ignored me. "Totally useless. Good for nothing. On the scrap heap at twenty-five. Seriously, I'm worried about you."

One of John's more attractive traits is that ever since I have known him he has been worried about me. He is concerned for my health, lectures me on my drinking habits, though no mean performer himself in this line, and points out the cost of my overdraft.

"What about that money you're coming into?" John asked.

"I'll get round to that in due course. It was mine when I was twenty-one. But if you can recollect I was somewhere in the Middle East at the time. No doubt the Old Man will mention it in due course."

John was referring to some money left to me in trust by my grandfather.

"How much is it?" he asked.

"Seven or eight thousand pounds."

"That'll hardly see you through a dirty week-end today," he remarked.

"Yes, that's a bore. When I was at school I looked forward to the day when I could go and live in Paris off the income from it, and be a great poet."

"That you will never be. Maybe a great piss-artist," said John. "Anyway, I can see nothing will make you change your mind. You're determined to make as big a prick of yourself in Civvy Street as you did in the army. And you won't have me around to pick up the pieces."

We stayed in the rapids until a cool breeze began to blow along the valley. We dressed and drove back to my father's house.

John produced another bottle of whiskey from his car. This had the most profound effect on my father. For the remaining thirty years of his life he never forgot John Fish.

"Charming fellow," he would say whenever we got round to discussing old times. "Very charming fellow. Must bring him down again sometime. You were lucky to have such a decent chap to keep an eye on you during the last Brew Up."

Where he got the idea that John Fish kept an eye on me, I shall never know. It is arguable that my military career might have been considerably more successful if I had not had the good fortune to spend so much of it with John. But as I have written before, whereas John had a remarkable knack of extracting himself from awkward situations, once I got into them I was always right in them up to my neck.

# 4

I returned to London the following day. My first problem was to find myself accommodation. After wandering round the streets of the West End and proffering folding money to hall porters and receptionists, by lunch time I had had no success.

I had begun to wonder how anyone procured a room, and was almost on the point of trying my luck at the Gladstone, when I happened to be passing the Green Park Hotel. On enquiring at Reception I was told that I would be allowed a room with a bed for four nights only.

Having paid about twenty pounds in advance I was somewhat shocked at the state of the room. It was scrupulously clean, but badly in need of refurnishing. The carpet was worn through to the boards, and the furniture should long ago have been chopped up for firewood. As for the bed, I can only say if it could have talked it would have told a tale of unspeakable lechery. Such springs as remained reacted noisily when I sat on it. But I was delighted at having secured a base. I felt childishly pleased with myself, and it seemed to me that all that was required in Civvy Street was the ability to persevere.

The time had now come to renew such contacts as I had left behind me in London more than four years ago, when I had last been on leave there. The trouble was that I had no address book, but I reckoned that if I could see just one of my old friends, very quickly I would be drawn into the orbit of the others.

The trouble was that I could recall very few names. What I had forgotten was that, during the years I had been in the forces, I had looked back with longing and nostalgia at a way of life, rather than at individual people. I should explain here that, before I had been called up early in 1941, I had been a journalist first on a provincial paper and then on a national Sunday. I had thought of myself as a poet, certainly as a writer, and I had seen the last days of the Cafe Royal, and moved in somewhat exalted circles. This had been due to my friendship with Stephen Spender and Peter Watson who supplied the financial backing to the magazine *Horizon* which was edited by Cyril Connolly. Through Peter and Stephen I had met a considerable number of people. There seems little point in giving names, and if I mention a few it is in the cause of name-dropping. But it had been very exciting for a young man like myself to have met Graham Sutherland, Henry Moore, George Orwell, Hugh Walpole, Eddie Marsh, Christopher Isherwood, W. H. Auden, Cecil Day Lewis, John Lehmann, Edith Sitwell, Frederick Ashton and Margot Fonteyn, Sir Osbert Sitwell, Laurie Lee, Herbert Read, among many others. I very much doubt if any of these that are still alive would even remember me. If they do they would undoubtedly recall a young pseudo-intellectual much given to sounding off about matters about which he knew nothing. Still, that is the prerogative of youth when you can get away with it. You certainly cannot do so in middle age.

After several wrong numbers and no replies, I eventually got through to John Lehmann. If I remember correctly he had just about moved into his house in Egerton Crescent in Knightsbridge. John is one of the people with whom I have retained a tenuous contact over the years. He was at that time an editor of importance. He had always been a very good friend to me, and even went so far as to publish some of my poetry in one of his magazines.

I had got to know John well during the three months prior to my call up. I had been very broke at the time and had worked for him at the Hogarth Press for about three months. It was during this time that Virginia Woolf committed suicide. I met her on several occasions but she showed no liking for me. This did not upset me at the time, as I considered it her misfortune, and always found her arrogant. She is, I know, considered a great writer but I have never been able to finish one of her books.

During my years overseas John had been one of the few people who had taken the trouble to keep in touch with me. I do not mean that he wrote me long letters. They may only have been a few words but they were at least some kind of contact with the world that I had been forced to abandon. I understand that he wrote to a great number of people in the forces, especially if they were overseas, and I think that he liked to think of himself as a kind of cultural father figure. And although he himself did not serve in the forces, he wrote war-slanted editorials in his magazine under the title of "The Armoured Writer." These were more acceptable to his friends in the forces than the "Comments" that Cyril Connolly wrote in *Horizon*. The trouble with the latter was that he was continually lamenting the state of the writer in wartime. It seemed to him wrong that the wretched writer should be denied the fruits of the South of France, the best clarets, not to mention an adequate supply of food to give him strength to wield his pen. I never discovered how serious Cyril Connolly was when he appealed to his American fellow writers to dispatch food parcels to the London Office of *Horizon* to alleviate the starvation rampant among England's writers. But I have a feeling that however much people laughed at him and he laughed at himself, there was an underlying seriousness to his appeals.

Half an hour after I had spoken to John on the telephone, he had answered the door and led me into his library.

The most important thing about that meeting with John was that the first thing he did was to offer me some practical help by way of accommodation.

I had no idea of the magnitude of the problem for it had not occurred to me that as a result of the bombing of London and the fact that no rebuilding had taken place during the war years, not to mention the flux of people returning or just bent on pleasure, all types of accommodation were at a premium.

But that day in August 1946 John had heard through a friend of his that there was a single flat available in a block in Jermyn Street. And in order to secure it for me then and there, he telephoned his friend to ask him to raise heaven and hell to get hold of it for me. It was arranged that I should go round that same evening and have a word with the caretaker. It appeared that a small sweetener would be required to pass from my hand into his. This came as no surprise to me.

Nor was I surprised when John asked me what I was going to do. I had grown to expect it from everyone I met, and I gave the usual answer that I proposed to have a look around.

This drew the usual response. "You'll find things have changed quite a lot, Michael. Have you ever thought of going up to university? You can get a full grant to go there for three years with your amount of war service. It would give you a chance to find your feet, and at the same time you could work for a degree. I think they're still going to be in demand."

I was appalled at the thought of a further three years incarceration at a university.

I thanked John for his advice, and reaffirmed that it was my intention to have a look around and get the lie of the land. We arranged to meet at a later date and I departed in the direction of Jermyn Street to secure myself a more permanent base from which I could conduct operations.

My luck was in. Ten five pound notes were exchanged and I found myself the tenant of a one room flat for the sum of seven pounds a week. It was considerably more cheerful than my room at the Green Park Hotel, besides having the advantage of a small kitchen. The worst part about it was the exterior of the building, which like all other buildings in London was in need of a coat of paint. It had also received a near miss from a bomb and was propped up by large lumps of wood and steel girders. But the outside did not worry me. I was excited beyond belief to have secured a base, from which I could emerge daily to explore London with all the possibilities that it held in store for me.

After the deal had been satisfactorily concluded, I made my way to the Ritz to pick up the civilian clothes which I had left there with the hall porter. I looked in at the bar, but seeing no one I knew, had one drink and returned to my new flat. As usual I noticed, now that the evening was getting on, that hordes of tarts of all sizes shapes and ages had poured into Piccadilly to solicit for custom. Jermyn Street was the same, but to my experienced eye, it seemed that here was a slightly higher class of whore. But declining all offers and temptations I fought my way back to the flat where I deposited my gear.

I then lay down on my bed debating what I should do to celebrate my third evening back in the old country. I would dearly have loved to meet someone with whom I could have talked. My telephone in the room was not working, so I went downstairs to find a telephone box.

The first one on the corner of the road that ran through to Piccadilly was engaged by two soldiers, who appeared to be embracing one another. I asked them politely if they could find somewhere else to do their courting. They seemed to find this amusing and left without abusing me. I went inside and dialled Peter Watson's number.

My call to Peter was successful, although he sounded surprised and not particularly elated at hearing my voice. I was a little shocked too when he said "I haven't seen you for years. Have you been away?" So much so for my peregrinations throughout the Middle East and the intemperate climate of Italy in defence of democracy and *Horizon* magazine, which as I have said he financed. However, he asked me to lunch with him the following day.

The rest of my evening in the West End was unmemorable and no different from those that I had spent on leave there in the past. There were vast crowds, still mostly servicemen, pubs packed to the doors with everyone fighting for drink, or one another. The atmosphere did not seem so friendly as in the past, but I attributed this to the desperate shortage of drink, and the maniacal desire of millions of people to lay their hands on it. Shortages usually produce short tempers, and there was no shortage of them that night.

At one point I found myself at the French Pub in Dean Street. Here were a number of Free French sailors, with a posse of homosexuals in close pursuit. I admired the way the former accepted drink after drink from the latter. I did not have the slightest doubt that when the time came to deliver the goods the only orifice they would disappear up would be their own.

At one point I thought I recognized a familiar face, so I fought my way towards it. But as I was about to address its owner he turned his back on me and continued an animated conversation with his companions. I have always been shy by nature, so I turned away and made another foray in the direction of the bar. Suddenly the pub began to empty at a remarkable speed. It reminded me of the out of bounds bars in Italy which would be packed to the doors one moment, but as soon as the Military Police so much as put their noses in the vicinity, would be vacated by soldiers of all nations who had developed antennae finely tuned to the presence of M.Ps. I was about to prepare myself for a dive under the nearest table in the event of hostilities, when I realized that the exodus was due to the supply of booze drying up at source. Remembering the advice as to what to do if I ever got lost in Venice, namely to follow the crowd, I did just that. Attaching myself to its tail I followed it a few yards along Old Compton Street. A howl of disappointment went up, when its leaders saw attached to the door of the Swiss Pub a NO DRINK sign. The crowd immediately disintegrated into smaller groups, who after going into huddles, set off to various public houses in distant parts in the hope of finding some kind of refreshment.

I was not exactly despondent, but the idea of hunting like packs of wolves in pursuit of booze seemed to me undignified. So after trying my luck round several more Soho pubs, and securing the prize of a small whiskey in one of them at the Oxford Street end of Wardour Street, I decided to return to my base in Jermyn Street.

Business was brisk as I made my way along it, and bargains were being struck on all sides, without too much hesitation on the principle that those who hesitated were lost since demand heavily outnumbered supply. I seated myself in the window of a small cafe half way along the street to survey the scene. I was now becoming more acclimatized to the Old Country's shortcomings, and was not duly upset when my request for a plate of bacon and eggs was met with a look of dumb insolence by a plain girl, who was more interested in keeping an eye on the street market outside. Judging from the quality of some of the girls out there, it was a mystery why she had not thrown in her hand at being a waitress, to which clearly she was not suited by temperament, and joined their ranks. Having asked for a menu, and having been laughed at as if I were an imbecile escaped from a lunatic asylum, I was finally proffered a plate of savoury mince. I have never been able to look any kind of mince in the face since. Even mince in a butcher's window is apt to bring on acute nausea. This house speciality was accompanied by a cup of unsweetened tea. If my drivers had been served it by my Corporal cook, he would never have lived to see another day. I was fascinated to discover what it contained. I sipped it and poured some of its contents into the saucer in an attempt to analyse it. My conclusions were so disgusting that I paid my bill and left.

When I entered the main door of my bombed block of flats, I realized straight away in what kind of an institution I had been lucky enough to find accommodation. I have always been brothel prone, in the same way as certain people are accident prone. I have been very saddened recently to read of all the destruction that has been wrought in the beautiful city of Beirut, in the name of God and politics. I was journeying down from the desolation of Iraq where I had been guarding an evil-smelling pipe line sometime in 1942, when I decided to allow the convoy I commanded to proceed South to Egypt in the capable hands of my Sergeant, while I branched off with Driver Lane at the wheel of my fifteen hundredweight to savour the fleshpots of Beirut.

Funds were low at the time. Although Driver Lane had done good business with the wogs of Iraq by flogging them dried tea leaves, the income from this industry had only been sufficient to cover my gambling debts in the Officers Mess. Needless to say, my losses had been John Fish's gain. Accordingly, not wishing to be crippled with the expense of a luxury hotel, and anticipating that I should in any case be spending most of my days and nights in the lowest dives I could search out in my limited time, I paid a call on the Town Major with a request to supply me with a list of the cheapest hotels.

The Town Major kindly obliged. I looked down the list and chose the one at the bottom which was the cheapest. It was called the Hotel Mimosa. Driver Lane was upset. He did not consider it worthy of my status. I pointed out to him that none of my brother Officers was present, and there was no need to inform them of this shameful act of economy on my part. Furthermore, I reminded him that our shortage of cash was due to his failure to open up further avenues of income during our stay in the wilds of Iraq. When he countered by asking me what I had done to increase my poor pay as an Officer, and his disgraceful remuneration as a mere driver, I indicated that it was not my duty as someone who had been granted a commission by His Majesty to meddle in anything so sordid as trade; what was more, that if he failed to acquit himself more successfully in the future in the replenishment of our drought-ridden coffers, maybe he would care to return to being an ordinary driver, to cease to receive my protection as my batman, to return to those vital duties of twenty-four hour guards, fire pickets, night pickets, early morning parades, to mention just a few of the obligations that a true driver was called upon to fulfil.

After my homily I never heard a further word of reprimand from Driver Lane. What is more he set his mind to fulfilling my financial commitments. Even when we left Beirut he had managed to obtain a few bundles of Syrian pounds. Not as negotiable as gold, but still it was an encouraging start and I was pleased that my words of warning had not gone unheeded.

The Hotel Mimosa was delightful. It was a brothel. I am most grateful to the Town Major for recommending it. It was scrupulously clean, and the girls were beautiful. I immediately struck up a rapport with the Madam, who introduced me to one of her most charming workers. I negotiated a cut price rate for my stay of five days. I do not know why Madam treated me so well. Perhaps it was on account of my youth. But she went to the trouble of packing up a luncheon basket for two each day. My girl and I would take this to a deserted sandy beach and spend the day there sunbathing, drinking and eating, returning to the hotel in the evening for a preliminary bout of love, before going out to dine.

As I climbed the stairs of the apartment in Jermyn Street I was nearly knocked down on several occasions by girls hurling themselves down in pursuit of further customers in the street, or by those dragging their freshly found clients upstairs with a view to getting through the business with maximum speed. It seemed to me undignified, and feeling no inclination to partake of this meat market, I went into my room and locked the door.

My night was disturbed. To begin with the pounding of feet continued until three in the morning. This was varied by screams, shouts of abuse, and thumpings. As the walls of the apartments were made of the flimsiest three-ply, I was able to lie awake listening to the most hair-raising sexual projects being discussed by the girl who operated on my right. To my left was a keen flagellant, who showed no mercy to her clients, whose shouts of ecstatic pain were a credit to the skill with which she wielded her whips. I also heard performed an act of such gross indecency that I do not dare to write it here in case I should be prosecuted for corrupting the youth of the nation. It was, as Coleridge wrote, "A thing to dream of, not to tell."

As a result of my disturbed night, I was feeling tired, when I reached the Pinnochio Restaurant in Dean Street, where I had arranged to meet Peter Watson for lunch.

Peter was already seated at the table.

His first remark was: "No, it can't be you. It just can't be." This welcome was followed by a clucking in the throat, a cross between a cough and a laugh and a sure sign that he was amused.

"My, my, haven't you grown enormous. I wonder if that chair will hold your weight? Perhaps we ought to ask one of the waiters to find you something a little more solid. You see everything's very delicate in here. Nothing old English about this place. It's absolutely *nouvelle vague*. Rather chic, don't you think?"

I looked round the restaurant and had to admit that it was something different. In a few years time hundreds like it designed by fashionable Italians would spring up all over London. Decor in due course would become more important than food. The restaurant owners that had the good sense to combine both were to make fortunes.

As soon as I had ordered my food I asked Peter to give me all the news. He seemed to find this request amusing because it produced a further outburst of clucking.

"A lot of water has flowed under the bridges since I saw you. What do you want to know about?"

"Tell me about *Horizon* and Cyril Connolly for instance."

"They are both costing me an absolute fortune," he said. "I do not think I can afford either for much longer. Cyril is out of his mind. He seems to think I am a Bank. He lives in the utmost splendour surrounded by ladies, the best claret and vintage port. He sallies forth to the finest restaurants and will only be seen riding in the new taxis that have just appeared on the streets. We will go and visit him later. Perhaps if we are very polite he will offer us a sip of champagne. He's the only person who has an unlimited supply of the stuff in England, and if I remember correctly you used to be very fond of it."

"I don't think Cyril likes me very much," I said.

The coolness between Cyril and myself had taken place sometime in 1940. He had not been pleased when Peter had suggested that I might do some book reviewing for *Horizon*. But as Peter held the moneybags he had acquiesced ungraciously, and who shall blame him? I did a very bad review of a novel by Henry Yorke. This was the last time that I was to appear in print in *Horizon*.

One day Peter brought back a bunch of grapes to the *Horizon* office which in those days was in Stephen Spender's flat in Landsdowne Terrace, Bloomsbury. The sight of these grapes had sent Cyril into ecstasy, and during the afternoon his hand had kept wandering towards them, so that by the evening he had consumed the entire bunch.

Some days later I had written Peter a letter, and at the bottom had drawn a crude picture of a chimpanzee holding a bunch of grapes to his mouth. I had written beside it "Who is this? It must be the Chump or the Chimp."

This letter had fallen into Cyril's hands. I have not the slightest doubt that Peter left it intentionally on his desk. This is not to be malicious about Peter or to speak evil of him now that he is dead. Peter loved gossip, and was prone to stirring up trouble between his friends and acquaintances. I think he was amused how easily people could become upset with one another over the pettiest reasons.

Cyril took my art very much to heart and ever since the incident we had only exchanged the time of day. Needless to say all my future contributions to the magazine came back with a rejection slip. I am sure they were not up to his high standards anyway.

"The trouble is that I am no longer a rich man," Peter informed me. "My income has been halved in the last five years, and the government is determined to get its hands on to what is left."

Before the war Peter had a flat in Paris. Although I had never visited it, I knew that it contained a collection of pictures. I asked him what had happened to them.

"Looted by the Germans and the French, of course," he said.

I sensed that I was having a depressing effect on him. I also realized half an hour after I had joined him, that he was not interested in my past, my heroic deeds in the Middle East and Italy, and still less in my future.

Trying to change the subject I asked him what had happened to Stephen Spender.

This question again produced the sound of chuckling. "Stephen never does anything these days but rush from one conference to another. You can't open *The Times* today without seeing his name among a list of protesters writing about some injustice or other. You know he spent some time during the war as a fireman? Too bizarre for words."

When we had finished luncheon, Peter suggested that I accompany him on his visit to Cyril. I accepted out of curiosity. We took a taxi to a grand house near Regent's Park. Outside Peter paused, looked up, and commented: "Only the best for our Cyril. But I don't know how long he thinks I can afford to go on paying the bills. He's crazy, absolutely out of his mind."

Cyril Connolly was certainly doing himself proud. We found him stretched out on a chaise longue in the first floor drawing-room. Paying court to him were two pretty girls. One was holding a glass of champagne to his mouth, while the other was standing by with liberal helpings of caviare spread on dry biscuits ready to place them between his lips at his command.

Cyril was clearly not pleased to receive *in flagrante delicto*, and demanded who had let us in.

"Your butler," said Peter.

"Haven't got a butler," said Cyril. But the idea of a butler appealing to him, he added. "Perhaps I should engage a butler. What do you think, Peter? We could put him on the pay role and use him at *Horizon* parties. That would make him chargeable to tax, wouldn't it?"

Up to now Cyril had ignored me. When Peter introduced me, he nodded in my direction. Either he did not remember me, or did not want to.

I felt out of place. I drank a glass of champagne and, having arranged to meet Peter again, I said good-bye and left.

Both Cyril and Peter were part of the pre-war artistic and literary establishment which was to hold power until the early seventies, by which time their numbers were thinned by the reaper. They were part of an establishment which I was to grow to dislike. Possibly this antipathy towards them had its roots in the day I saw them thirty years ago.

Fellow members of the same group had lived in many cases very agreeable lives during the twenties, when the pound dominated the international money markets, and one could live abroad like a king on an income of £250 a year. Life was easy for would-be writers and artists in those days. Many of them had small private incomes, and those who did not could look to patrons for hand-outs when times were rough. It was a small and tight-knit group, all of whom knew each other. Their lives, loves and hates were, generally speaking, confined to their own circle. The world outside passed by unheeded and uncared for. In the thirties the leaders were drawn for the most part from the Bloomsbury group.

The day after my lunch with Peter and my visit to Cyril Connolly, I decided that before I did anything else I would organize myself further to facilitate my return to Civvy Street. As I was not much pleased with the suit I had been issued with at Aldershot, I took the bus to Harrods. It is interesting to recall that my choice of store in those days was Harrods. This was an hangover from the pre-war days, when my family had automatically shopped for everything at Harrods where they all had accounts. They would never have thought of going elsewhere. You could almost say that they were born there. They were certainly buried by Harrods' undertaking department. I had my first money box supplied by Harrods and it was a diabolical contraption. Once money had been consigned to it, there was no way of making it disgorge. One day I became so enraged with it, that I battered it flat with a sledge hammer. For this offence my father beat me. What made the beating particularly painful was that although I had reduced the box to pulp, not a penny did I succeed in extracting from it. I detested that money box. Every shilling I was given I was compelled to feed into its jaws. Spending money in those days was a crime. To spend capital was on a par with raping one's sister. Money was made to be saved. When the box was full I would take it to the main hall at Harrods where there was a children's bank. There, with tears in my eyes, I would watch that hateful box being opened with a key, its contents counted, and paid into my account. Once lodged with Harrods I could say good-bye to them for ever, because only with my father's permission and signature, could I lay my hands on them and there was no chance of that happening. I am not quite sure what I was saving for. Perhaps I was compelled to be thrifty with a view to providing for my old age. I was certainly not saving to buy something I really wanted. My brother and I had a monumental row with our father when my brother was seventeen and I was sixteen. With much love and labour we had built a hydroplane. To power it we found a sixteen-horse-power secondhand outboard motor, whose owner was asking fourteen pounds. When we suggested to our father that this sum could come out of our savings with Harrods, he looked at us as if we intended to commit some major crime. In no way was he prepared to countenance what he called such flagrant extravagance.

I was shocked when I entered Harrods that morning, shocked because there was so little merchandise on display. (The food department had been my favourite area as a boy.) Empty shelf after empty shelf met my gaze. Gone were the hundreds of hams from all parts of Britain, each one cured to the local recipe. On the cheese counter there was only a pile of two-ounce pieces of an indifferent looking cheddar. Not a sign of creamy Camemberts, whole Stiltons or the large Bries laid out on straw. Yet there was no shortage of customers. Indeed they were of exactly the same breed as during the pre-war days. There were two kinds, the town and the country customers, the latter identifiable by their sensible brogues and tweed skirts. There was no question of anyone paying cash. As each one took his two-ounce ration of cheese carefully wrapped in grease proof paper, the man serving them would enter the purchase into a book.

Somewhat dazed, I found my way to the man's department, even more conspicuous by the absence of anything on show for sale.

I asked for a suit and was conducted by the salesman to a cupboard in the corner of the department, which he proceeded to open with a flourish. This was pure showmanship on his part, a hangover from more fruitful days, because among the hundred or so suits on display there was only one of my size. It was made of grey flannel, of a very much superior quality to the one the army had issued me with. I tried it on, and looking at myself in the mirror, I found it extraordinary how considerably it changed my personality. Gone was that somewhat battered military look, to be replaced by a nondescript citizen. I asked how much it was and was appalled to be told that it was fifteen pounds. The same suit would have cost five pounds in 1939. I was to discover that to be the average rate of inflation since the pre-war days.

"May I have your book of clothing coupons, Sir?" asked the salesman.

Unfortunately I had forgotten to bring them with me. Automatically my hand went to my pocket, and I slid forward a one pound note.

The salesman was shocked. "But this is Harrods, sir," he exclaimed, drawing back from me as if I were a pariah.

This reaction on his part dumbfounded me. All I could think of saying at this unexpected rebuff was: "Then what are we going to do?"

"May I suggest, sir, that you pay for the suit and leave it here, and come back with your coupons?" He paused. "That is, Sir, if you still want the suit."

"Of course I want it," I said huffily.

I left Harrods in a slight daze, and went into the nearest pub to wash my wounds.

I returned with my clothing coupons later that day, and collected the grey flannel suit. Strangely enough I found myself in no haste to put it on. I continued to wear my bedraggled battle dress for the next three months at least. It was most extraordinary considering how I had longed to be a civilian once again. It was as if there was some mysterious force at work, impeding my crossing back to Civvy Street.

# 5

Although there were cooking facilities in my flat in Jermyn Street, during my first week in London I ate out in restaurants of various types. I found that the cheaper the place, the more meagre and disgusting the food. I was surprised to find how seriously the Government took rationing. In order to give the impression that everyone, rich and poor alike, was suffering equally, it had decreed that the maximum amount that could be charged for a meal was five shillings. Today that sounds ridiculous, but in 1946 five shillings went a long way and must be the equivalent of two pounds today if one takes inflation into consideration.

If the Government was determined, according to its socialist principles, that all should bear an equal burden, few people did so. The expensive restaurants ignored it, and fiddled the bills. The usual way round this bit of unenforceable legislation was to enter the amount spent over five shillings under the heading of drinks. While the food was inedible in cheap cafés, it was abundant and delicious in all the posh restaurants. One would never have known that there had been a war on, and I felt much more at home when I was eating the best that the Black Market could provide. It was a mystery to me why everything should be in such short supply, and I felt resentful towards a Government that seemed to be revelling in austerity instead of doing its best to relieve the gloom and get the lights on with maximum speed. I was positively aghast when bread rationing was introduced after the war, something that had not even been thought necessary during England's darkest hours. It seemed to me that the Government was incompetent.

I soon discovered that there was a Black Market for everything that was rationed or in short supply. The laws of supply and demand operated in exactly the same way as they had done in Italy. Few people thought it immoral to buy in the Black Market, least of all the three and a half million members of the forces who had been hastily demobilized. If there is one thing in service life that is of benefit to the individual, it is a thorough grounding in the art of scrounging. You could say that the entire country in 1946 was on the fiddle. Every new regulation was promulgated to be evaded.

I wined and dined several times in solitary state at the Etoile restaurant, which had been one of my favourites before the war, when it had also been a small hotel, and where one could stay for five shillings a night. Now it was much grander, the haunt of successful actors, agents and publishers who love to eat well while their writers starve. Here I was able to consume the most tender steaks, the most fancy hors-d'oeuvres, and puddings and pies covered with lashings of cream. And it was not expensive. A four course meal with a bottle of good wine would cost about four pounds, and this would include a few strong drinks beforehand and several brandies afterwards, vital for settling the stomach.

I quickly came to an understanding with a butcher and a grocer just off Jermyn Street that I was not interested in mastering the intricacies of a ration book. Indeed the food that the ration book supplied seemed to me insufficient for survival, although all around me I saw people looking fitter than they had ever looked before. This may have been due to the fact that in the pre-war days a great number of people had eaten far too much, excepting the country's two million unemployed who were on a starvation diet. Or it may have been due to free issues of rose-hip jelly and halibut oil to the youth of the nation. I made it absolutely clear to my friend the butcher after the necessary financial transaction had taken place, that I was no lover of sausages stuffed with bread and that if anyone was going to be lumbered with the fatty bits of meat it was not to be me. A similar agreement was reached with the grocer. I made it clear that soapy cheddar was not to come my way, and that any supplies of Camembert or Brie that were smuggled in from France were to find their way into my basket. I was well served by both. They liked me because I never queried their bills. I had learned under Driver Lane's expert tuition that the one thing that Black Marketeers cannot stand from their clients is any sign of meanness.

It must have been about this time that I came to the conclusion that if one wanted to make money, the sure way to do so was on the Black Market. In the back of my mind was planted the idea that I could do no better than join in the game and gather some of the rich pickings. On all sides I could see Black Marketeers, and they were obviously rich, successful and pleased with themselves. They gathered on street corners, in bars and in the most expensive restaurants and hotels. They were identifiable by their Savile Row suits and silk shirts, and their girls who were beautiful and sported the latest thing in nylon stockings which were retailing at eight pounds a pair under the counter. These marketeers came from all kinds of backgrounds. There was a sprinkling of pre-war spivs, smart youngsters from London's East End and from South of the river, a leavening of ex-servicemen, and at the top a few big time crooks who were driven round in large cars by uniformed chauffeurs. Needless to say, these last named were responsible for sweetening the upper echelons of the police, and seeing that from the top to the bottom of the Force everyone was properly looked after. I think this disregard for the law was the most remarkable effect the war had had on the population of Britain.

I was happy during my first week in Jermyn Street, even if my nights were disturbed by the comings and goings of the girls with their clients. It was during my stay there that I first became aware of the large number of boys who were on the game much to the annoyance of the girls who did not like to watch their potential income being poached. The favourite pick-up places of these boys were the public urinals which existed in far greater numbers in London's West End than they do today. There was a particularly famous one, a favourite haunt of the queers of all nations near the Ivy Restaurant. When the day came for it to be dismantled, it was bought by a rich American who transported it to his palace in Hollywood where he had it erected at the bottom of his garden. Here he would indulge in the sport of picking up boys, whom he specially hired to entertain him and his fellow guests.

In 1946 these "Cottages", as urinals were known in the trade, were extremely dangerous even to visit, however innocent one might be and however urgent the call of nature. For whereas the police turned a blind eye to the extensive operations of the Black Market, queers were there for bashing and arresting at the slightest provocation. To further the number of arrests they would send *agents provocateurs* around these cottages particularly favoured by homosexuals. Here they would stand for hours pretending to pee, waiting for a look or an open invitation from some unfortunate queer. By these disgraceful methods they were able to arrest hundreds of homosexuals daily, and in many cases these unfortunate people were sent to prison for long stretches. No one was immune.

Famous actors, members of Parliament, dignitaries of the Church, lions of Fleet Street were all caught red-handed and heavily fined or trundled off to prison. What amazed me is why the queers still persisted in visiting these perilous spots, which were both smelly and unhygienic. I am told that it was the element of danger that added spice to their quests. I suppose it's this that adds that something extra to climbing mountains or hang gliding.

As I began to feel my way through the intricate highways and byways of Civvy Street, my days took on some kind of routine. About eleven o'clock, or to be more honest, at opening time, I would make my way to the Salisbury next door to what was then called the New Theatre in St Martin's Lane. The Salisbury was a Free House, and owned by an old friend of mine, George Holmes, whom I had known in the Middle East when he had been a lance corporal in charge of the NAAFI truck. The NAAFI was responsible for supplying the troops with everything from booze to buttons. Many hard things were said about it and its initials were variously interpreted from Never 'Ave Any Fags In, to No Ambition And Fuck-all Interest.

George had already been back in England for a year, and his pub was doing a roaring trade.

At the Salisbury I met my oldest friend of Civvy Street days, David Kentish. He was Production Manager for Laurence Olivier at the New Theatre next door to the pub. I had known David from my school days at Bryanston, from which we had both been expelled on the charge that we were not cooperative. Since then he had always wanted to be a painter, but through necessity and family commitments he drifted first into the theatre and later on into television.

David introduced me to Laurence Olivier who at the time was married to Vivien Leigh. I had of course seen her in *Gone With the Wind* and was shortly to see her on the stage in Thornton Wilder's pretentious *The Skin of Our Teeth*. She was a superb actress and one of the most beautiful women I have ever met. Olivier himself was already at the top of his profession. David was devoted to him, and on the few occasions that I met Olivier he made me feel that I was somebody, not just another piece of flotsam thrown up on the tide lines of Civvy Street.

To return to my routine. At opening time I would present myself at the Salisbury and proceed to drink four or five large Scotches with George Holmes. In the course of these sessions I gradually enlarged my circle of friends, or perhaps I should say acquaintances. Sometimes David would join us, but he always drank the excellent Flowers Keg Bitter, which George kept on draught. This was real bitter and not the pressurized gaseous liquid which is associated with the word keg today.

One day David announced that he intended to get married. The wedding was attended by both Olivier and Vivien Leigh, and was a success except that present at the booze up after the ceremony was David's first girl friend with whom he had lived for many years. It was in their house that I had spent my embarkation leave before departing in tears to roam the globe in defiance of Hitler. I was very fond of her, and she gave me the impression that she viewed David's marriage with considerable scepticism.

David and his bride committed the error of tempting fate. While they were photographed with Olivier, they also insisted on being photographed indoors under an unfurled umbrella. This, as all occultists know, is asking for trouble. In due course they were divorced.

I wracked my brains as to what I should give the bride and bridegroom. There was very little in the shops worth buying. Indeed I had by now almost entirely given up the practice of going into them since I found it much easier to deal on the Black Market. Among my acquaintances with whom I drank at the Salisbury were several eminent marketeers who came up with various suggestions, ranging from a crate of Scotch to a recently cured York Ham. But I decided that both of these were ephemeral, and I finally picked upon two sets of pink double cotton sheets. These cost considerably more than they would today even allowing for inflation, but did not of course call for any clothing coupons. By now I had decided that all rationing of whatever nature was an unnecessary irritant only to be disregarded.

One of George's main problems was to keep his pub supplied with liquor. He considered it careless to run out at any time, when there were thousands of customers clambering to hand their money over the bar. It was a classic example of too much money chasing too few goods. Accordingly he devoted a great deal of energy to establishing contacts throughout London who would keep him informed of the whereabouts of the stuff. One day I was greatly honoured when he asked me if I would be interested in accompanying him on a buying expedition. He had been tipped off that there had been a recent brew of sherry and red wine and that it was now, after a couple of days rest, suitably matured, and ready for consumption.

I think at this point George was seriously considering taking me in as a partner. In our dealings in the Middle East he must have appreciated my potential as a crook. I think he saw me, with my posh Oxford accent, as some kind of front man. As he once said to me it was quite extraordinary that someone as dishonest as myself had the right to go anywhere, into any hotel or restaurant, without being questioned by the doorman.

One morning, having consumed what George referred to as several heart-starters, we set off in a three ton lorry in an Easterly direction with George at the wheel. It was a fine day and, as we bowled through London, we burst forth in song. Among our repertoire was "When there isn't a girl you're on your only," which continues:

> You do feel lonely,
> Absolutely on the shelf
> Nothing to do but play with yourself,
> When there isn't a girl about.

Then we switched to the good ship Venus, memorable for the heinous crime of the cabin boy who:

> Stuffed his arse
> With broken glass
> And circumcized the skipper.

It was during that drive through London's East End that I began to have doubts as to whether Civvy Street was going to prove all that I had hoped it would be. Maybe it was being back in a cab that upset me. Maybe it reminded me of the days when I had been a driver at the beginning of the war. Maybe it induced nostalgia for the days in the Middle East and Italy when I had been cared for by my platoon of drivers, and even if times had been rough and the future unknown, I had never felt alone.

After about an hour's driving we went through Stratford East and turned off the main road, went down a side street, where we stopped in front of a broken down factory. George tooted the horn, the gates were flung open and we drove into the courtyard.

I thought I recognized the voice that called out: "Morning, Mr Holmes, Sir. Nice to see you again."

I got down from my side of the cab and recognized him immediately. It was my old batman Driver Tibbs, who had succeeded Driver Lane in that capacity, and proved a highly suitable choice. He had kept me supplied with more than adequate sums of money. It was he who had produced the quite admirable Lucia to be my friend and companion during my last week in Rome. With Lucia on my arm, I had put every General and Field Marshal to shame and made their companions look mere trollops. Tibbs and I had parted company after I had commanded the Italian Company near Salerno a year ago, and been sent to Naples to command a company of Germans, from whose midst I had so recently had to flee for fear of assassination by the Mafia.

"Fuck me, if it isn't Captain Nelson," said Tibbs, hurrying forward and shaking my hand. He seemed overcome and could only repeat "Fuck me." Finally recovering himself, he said "You look well, very well, Captain. When did you get back to Blighty?"

"A few weeks ago."

"Didn't take you long to get in to the rackets. Still the old Captain, I'm glad to see," said Tibbs. He turned to George. "Didn't know you were a friend of the Captain, Sir."

I quickly told Tibbs of my earlier association with George in the Middle East.

"Well, fuck me," said Tibbs. "It's a small world isn't it?" He turned to me. "You in on the vino racket then, Captain?"

"Michael's just having a day out with me," said George. "Look, why don't you two have a good natter and get it over with, while I go and get on with the business."

"You do that, Sir," said Tibbs. "Mr Williams is in the office waiting for you with the latest samples."

When George had left us, Tibbs again shook me by the hand and repeated his favourite two words, "Fuck me." Then he looked at me closely and said: "How you getting on, Captain? How are you finding life?"

"All right. Bit strange. Not exactly friendly. I suppose I thought I would receive a hero's welcome. But of course the war's been finished for over a year now, and everyone is getting on with their own thing."

"That's right, Captain. Most people couldn't care a tuppeney fart for us soldiers. I suppose we shouldn't have expected anything else. But it's every fucker for himself here now. Take me for instance. Went back to my old job as a metal polisher. Five fucking quid a week, and all the youngsters and shirkers promoted over my head. Fucking reserved occupations they called them, and the buggers were drawing quids a week while silly sods like you and me were on two bob a day."

I couldn't help smiling at the idea of Tibbs and myself on two shillings a day, when with his knowledge of the intricacies of the Italian Black Market, and my power as an Officer to smooth the path, we had lived like millionaires.

"I know what you're thinking," said Tibbs. "But those were the fucking spoils of war, weren't they? We had the right to them didn't we?"

"Certainly we did, Tibbs," I said.

It occurred to me that it was wrong for me to be calling him Tibbs, now that we were both civilians and equal, so I said: "What do I call you these days?"

"Just call me what you always called me, Captain. Tibbs or that idle fucking bastard. Anyway, don't let's stand here. Let's get a drink inside us." He turned and led the way into the factory.

In his cubby hole of an office he produced a bottle of whiskey and put it on the table. "Help yourself, Captain."

I poured a good measure into my glass and let out an exclamation of pleasure. It was a pure malt that Tibbs was offering me.

"Tibbs, you haven't changed," I said. "You're a bloody genius."

"Fifteen quid a bottle, Captain. Fifteen fucking quid, Captain, and they say we won the fucking war."

"So you're not working as a metal polisher any more?" I asked.

"Not bleeding likely. Jacked it in. Wrote to Mr Williams, I don't think you know him. Was my platoon commander in my mob while the war was on before I met you. Bloody nice man and a right piss artist. Always said I was to get in touch with him in Civvy Street if I wanted a job. Kept his word like a gentleman and so here I am, storekeeper in chief."

I couldn't help thinking that Mr Williams could employ no better storekeeper than Tibbs. There could be few sharp enough to outwit him.

"So you're in the wine trade," I said.

"Not exactly. The guvnor deals in everything. He calls himself an Importer and Exporter. Kind of covers everything from wine to women."

"White slaving included?" I asked.

"Not yet, Captain. But as long as the Yanks and all the other foreign buggers are still here, there will be a heavy demand for cunt. You must have noticed it in the West End. One fucking great brothel. Makes me sick to see all those ruddy foreigners playing about with our women. The guvnor's considering the situation. But if you ask me, the market has already been coined by the Sicilians and the Malts. I reckon there's going to be trouble. Having come through the last lot I don't want to end up with a knife in my guts. Still, if you reckon you're tough enough, a little brothel business would be the thing to invest in. Definitely."

In the course of further conversation I gathered that Mr Williams dealt in almost everything for which there was a demand. It appeared that not all of his business was crooked. In fact it seemed to me the line between honesty and crime had become blurred in post-war Britain. Excessive and repressive legislation had produced a crop of bureaucrats to enforce the law. They in turn had generated a host of petty criminals bent on evading it. Tibbs attributed a great deal of the trouble to the rise of the Socialists to power in Parliament. According to him they were a miserable lot of buggers who did not want anyone to have more fun than anybody else. He particularly disliked their belief that all men were equal.

"Look, Captain. No one was bloody equal in the bloody army. There's them that are born to command and them that are meant to obey." As an afterthought he added. "Forgive me for saying so, but there's an exception to every rule."

"How do you mean?"

"Don't take offence, Captain. There's yourself, for instance. The worst fucking Officer in the whole British army."

I think he saw how much his words had hurt me, for he added: "But I'll say something for you, Captain. You had enough bloody sense to leave us alone to get on with our thieving."

A few minutes later he had taken me into the office where we joined George and Freddie Williams. George was in high spirits, and I noticed that between them on the table was another bottle of malt whiskey, while on a trestle table down one side of the office were several rows of wine bottles. I examined them and was surprised to see that they were clarets and burgundies of pre-war vintage, all bearing the labels of a well-known wine shipper in St James's.

"How on earth did this stuff survive the war?" I asked. "Would you think it very rude of me if I could sample a bottle?"

This reasonable request of mine threw the other three into uncontrollable fits of laughter, which rather irritated me.

"I don't see anything particularly funny," I said. "It's a long time since I've tasted a decent French wine."

"I'm afraid most of us are in the same boat," said Freddie. He turned to Tibbs. "Pop along and bring up a bottle of the real stuff."

When Tibbs had left, Freddie said: "This is just our 'vin ordinaire.' Only for public consumption. No gentleman drinks it."

"What's the matter with it?" I asked.

"What's right with it?" said Freddie. "As a matter of fact this consignment is better than most. I don't think it will actually blind any of my customers though it will probably bring on the shits. A very smooth blending if I may say so. A basis of Algerian, with a mixture of scrumpy and elderberry, carefully sweetened with candy. No, not a bad brew."

"You've forgotten the colouring," said George.

"Ah, yes. The colouring. A good quality clotted blood," said Freddie.

"But the labels?" I said.

"A work of art aren't they?" said Freddie. He picked up a bottle and lovingly stroked the label.

George had taken out a bundle of notes and was counting them into piles of one hundred. "You strike a hard bargain, Freddie," he said.

"But where else could you find such labels?" said Freddie. "It's the labels you're paying for, not the piss inside."

A few minutes later Tibbs returned carefully nursing a bottle on its side. He handed the bottle to Freddie who showed us the label. "Now this is a very different kettle of fish. A fine label indeed, but inside nectar beyond praise. Gentlemen, Richebourg '37."

I could not help gasping with anticipatory pleasure. A man who could produce such a wine after the holocaust through which the world had passed was a genius indeed.

"It should of course have been allowed to stand and settle before decanting," said Freddie. "But seeing as how your friend Michael has but recently returned to these hostile shores, George, we cannot wait so long."

He picked up a cloth and carefully dusted the neck of the bottle.

"Oh, that reminds me, would you like the consignment dusted or not?"

"What do you think, Michael?" George said.

"Dusting, dusting ... I don't ..."

"Of course you wouldn't. It sort of adds verisimilitude, if that's the right word. Tibbs gets his staff to throw a little dust over the fresh brews. Gives them that look of age," said Freddie.

"That's right, Sir," said Tibbs. "Gives them a bit of class."

"I think dusted," said George.

"Very good sir. I'll get my men to load up your truck, sir. And dusted they shall be."

Tibbs shook me by the hand. "See you again, Captain. Keep out of trouble. Any real bother, give us a ring here."

I was still being paid by the army, and had some thousand pounds to my credit in the bank. So for the next month, certainly well into September I drifted about the West End of London, living a life of pleasure, keeping out of trouble, but gradually becoming bored and anxious about the future. I suppose there were thousands of young men and girls in the same position. They had looked forward to the day of their release from the forces, only to find that day not very much different from any other. Civvy Street turned out to be a bit of a flop.

During those weeks I never ceased to be amazed at the number of tarts operating throughout the West End. If I go on about this it is because of the enormity of the operation. Before the war they had of course solicited in the areas of Piccadilly and Shaftesbury Avenue, with the scrubbers working Charing Cross Road as far north as St Giles Circus.

I had as a young man in London before the war been attracted by tarts. At dusk on a summer's evening I would wander up and down Piccadilly listening to their cooings of enticement, praying that my cock would not split the seams of my trousers. It would take me a long time to pluck up courage to approach one, and even then I would often sheer away in fear, or else in the hope that the next one who accosted me would be more sexy or beautiful than the last. I think that in those days the tarts were on the whole more attractive than those operating in the immediate post-war years. The rule of quality and quantity applied. Certainly the pre-war girls were far cheaper. The going rate for a short time was one pound. For this the girl would masturbate you, and you were in and out of her room in five minutes flat.

In the following years, particularly overseas, I had recourse to a great number of whores. With rare exceptions, such as Lucia in Rome of whom I still dream, they were a thoroughly unpleasant lot. Quite rightly they despised their customers; they were only in the game for the money; they were often dirty and certainly the pros in Italy served the Fascists heroically and greatly impeded the Allied War Effort by handing out doses right and left.

If the Italian whores on the whole had been of poor quality and performance, I found the ones in my first weeks in Jermyn Street of an even lower standard. I have already said that the rules of quality and quantity together with those of supply and demand were operating. Those that I fancied were hotly pursued by hordes of lecherous military of all nations. The few that I managed to secure were in no way interested in giving value for money, at least not the kind of money that I was prepared to spend. Whereas a pre-war toss-off cost a pound, the price had now leapt outrageously to ten pounds. And woe betide any customer who failed to make it in that time. There was no question of money back either. Come in five minutes flat, or else out on the street. As to any finer and more refined delights, the cost of these were astronomical. An oral job was in the region of twenty pounds, and anything more imaginative required the resources of the Bank of England.

It was not until the day that the American forces returned to the States that the market collapsed and prices dropped to within the reach of the natives.

I found that apart from watching the activities of the tarts, my consumption of alcohol was rising and it had soon reached the level I was consuming prior to my undignified exit from Italy. Starting in the morning with George, I would get through at least a bottle of Scotch before lunch. This I often ate with George, and we went frequently to the Savoy Grill, where the wine cellars seemed to be recovering from the rigors of the war, although my palate was too jaded by that time to appreciate the finer vintages. In the afternoon George would retire to his bed and I would go to one of the innumerable drinking clubs that flourished round Piccadilly Circus. For the price of half a crown one became a member and could drink within the law until the pubs opened again at five-thirty. Many of these clubs had a high number of tarts among their members, but generally speaking it was considered to be non-gentlemanly to accost them when they came in off the streets to rest their aching feet and to have a livener between clients.

From five-thirty to closing time at eleven I would usually drink at the Salisbury, and my circle of acquaintances began to increase. Looking back I do not think I have known so many people in my life since. By closing time I would have downed another bottle of

Scotch. Still being young the thought of the loneliness of my one room flat in Jermyn Street did not appeal at all. Accordingly I would make a round of the night clubs.

These night clubs still flourished although the cost of going to them had risen considerably. In the pre-war days I had used a splendid night club called the Boogie-Woogie in Denham Street just off Piccadilly Circus. There had been no entrance fee, and the cost of a bottle of Scotch or gin had been one pound. This had been the general price. I believe that the Four Hundred was much more expensive, although I never went there because one had to be genuinely recommended for membership, and the wearing of evening dress was obligatory.

After several weeks of nosing around the various night clubs, I decided to settle for the Embassy in Bond Street as my nightly rendezvous. In the pre-war days it had been smart and frequented by such illustrious clients as the Prince of Wales and Mrs Simpson as she then was before she became the Duchess of Windsor. I had visited it during my one leave from Italy during the war, and had found it hospitable and helpful. I was particularly indebted to its two doormen who nightly assisted me into a waiting cab. They remained at the Embassy for many years, until it finally became a casino in the sixties, and they continued to afford me the same courtesy whenever I was the worse for wear.

One of the reasons for my picking the Embassy from the vast number of clubs available was that downstairs in the basement was a bar frequented by drunks like myself and a number of high-class tarts with a sprinkling of amateurs. Here one could drink to one's heart's content at very reasonable prices up to two in the morning, while the dancing and cabaret took place in the large room above.

In the course of the night I would chat up the pianist and get him to play all my favourite tunes. Nobody seemed to mind, as I leant in a state of inebriation across the piano staring into space as the melodies stirred up vague memories, some happy, at which my vacant face would twist into an idiot smile, some sad, at which the tears would roll down my grog-blossomed cheeks.

I made one or two attempts to get off with the girls. There was one from Yorkshire whom I much admired and whose accent fascinated me. The trouble was that they were all on duty until closing-down time, and there to extract as much cash as possible from the pockets of the customers. This is a universal practice the whole world over and consists of promising unmentionable delights in return for being bought drinks. The champagne is cider. the gin is water. The girls receive a commission on the number of drinks they cajole the customers into buying. The strange thing is that there was not a man in the place who was unaware of this and the fact that there was no leaving with the girls before closing time. Nevertheless they seem to love to be conned. When the time came to leave the place, most of them were too stoned out of their minds to know what they were doing, and the girls were able to elude their clutches and disappear to their homes alone without the burden of having to deliver the goods. I think the usual way of doing this was by leaving the drunken lecherous customer in the foyer while they repaired to the powder room, from which there was a private exit into the street. The strange thing is that the clients came back for more asset stripping.

Lest I give the impression of being above such foolery, let me say that the Yorkshire lass took every pound note off me on several occasions, having promised me unmentionable delights. I really fancied her, and like the rest of the poor sots there I believed that I and I alone would one day experience them. Perhaps after all I was amusing? Perhaps I was the first man that she really fancied?

Towards the end of September when I had been wandering round the West End in a semi-alcoholic state, enjoying myself less and less, I ran into my brother-in-law. He was considerably older than my sister and had married her in the course of the war. We lunched together at a restaurant in Holborn where now stands a metal and concrete box. I think he was perturbed to see the state I was in, being himself no stranger to the bottle. He was by way of being an accountant and he very kindly went through the list of his clients to see if any of them could be of use to me.

"I assume you want a job," he remarked.

"I suppose so," I answered. "But I'm not sure that I'm fit for anything."

"What about going back into newspapers?" he suggested. He must have learned from my sister that before the war I had worked as a reporter on the *Chichester Observer*, and then at the outbreak of war been lucky enough to move onto the *Sunday Pictorial*, now the *Sunday Mirror*, which was edited at the time by Hugh Cudlipp.

"Yes, that would be nice," I said. I did not add that I had never been any good as a reporter. I had been too shy. A good reporter has to be tough and skilled at getting his foot inside the door and keeping it there. I had hated the *Sunday Pictorial* and been scared to death of Hugh Cudlipp. While there I had spent most of my time answering letters on the John Noble Helping Hand Bureau. My job along with two other reporters was to answer readers' queries, and they had to be answered accurately. It might be a problem about bed bugs; it might be a query about a pension; or someone might write and complain of the quality and the price of a room where they had stayed. Each of these had to be researched, the persons involved contacted, from Ministry to individual, and where possible the complaint rectified. Personal letters were sent in reply, each one containing John Noble's best wishes and bearing his stamped signature.

Occasionally I would be dispatched on a story, but I usually returned empty handed and reported a non-story to a bemused News Editor, Sam Campbell, who very soon realized that I did not have, nor ever would have, within me the stuff that good reporters are made of. Shortly before going into the forces I left the paper.

So I was not very excited when my brother-in-law said that one of his clients worked at the Press Association and he would have a chat with him with a view to my getting a job there. I gave him my telephone number, not expecting to hear anything further from him, and forgot all about it.

When I was awakened a few days later with a hangover by the sound of the telephone ringing and had managed to raise enough strength to lift the receiver off the cradle, it took me at least a minute to remember why a secretary was asking me to go that morning to the P.A. building in Fleet Street to see a Mr Reynolds. I knew of no Mr Reynolds and in my condition that morning did not care much whether I met him or not, or anyone else for that matter. But the clouds drifted off my brain for a few seconds, and I remembered vaguely that my brother-in-law had mentioned the P.A., so I agreed to the meeting.

At eleven o'clock I presented myself at the P.A. building, having shaved, and cut myself, and donned my uniform whose Captain's pips on the shoulders were decidely tarnished. In due course I was ushered in to an inner office.

Behind the desk sat a giant of a man. As he rose to offer me his gorilla-like hand I estimated that he must have been seven feet tall. His face came from the same animal as his hand, and his paunch would have qualified for entry in the *Guinness Book of Records*, had it existed at the time.

When he had squeezed my hand to pulp he asked, or rather

growled at me to sit down.

"So you want a job." He said this as a statement of fact rather than as a question. Before I could say anything in reply, he continued "Experience?"

"*Sunday Pictorial* before service in the army."

"Why don't you go back? By law they're bound to have you."

"Left of my own accord before going into the army."

"Silly sod. Anyway, nothing for you here. Thousands of you buggers coming back and expecting work in Fleet Street. Take my advice and forget it."

"Thanks for the tip." I was piqued at being called for an interview to be told there was nothing for me. I felt like telling Mr Reynolds a few home truths about himself, but my sense of self preservation warned me not to tangle with a gorilla.

I was about to get up and leave, when Mr Reynolds said: "You could start as a junior sub on the sports desk tomorrow."

There are some historians who hold a theory that the future course of events can be affected by some relatively insignificant detail. For instance, Napoleon would have won the battle of Waterloo if he had not been suffering from a bad attack of piles at the time.

I think that if Mr Reynolds had not used that word *junior*, I would have accepted his offer, and the future of sports reporting in Fleet Street would have been of a far higher standard than it is today, and the commentaries on television would not sound like the work of lunatics recently released from mental institutions.

But the word *junior* stuck in my throat. In four and a half years, from the lowly rank of driver I had risen to the proud rank of Captain. And I was damned if I was going to be demoted to the rank of junior sub by some bloody civilian who had dodged the column. (I had no reason for supposing this. Indeed Mr Reynolds could for all I have known been a highly decorated Battle of Britain pilot.)

I held out my hand and said: "No, thank you, Mr Reynolds."

Mr Reynolds ignored my hand and me. Before I had reached the door he was back at his desk thumbing through a pile of flimsies.

There are few things that I regret in my life. I regret most of all that I did not see more of my mother when I was on leave from Italy at the end of the Italian campaign and before the war in the far East had been concluded by the dropping of the atomic bomb. I regret less, but still regret, that I did not take that job of junior sub on the sports desk at the Press Association.

It was now the beginning of October 1946, and the weather changed. It suddenly turned cold.

# 6

In the last thirty years remarkable claims have been made for the Ministry of Information by those who found within its bosom a haven from service in the forces. I am biased against it, because I was one of the less clever ones who failed to find refuge there. The British Council was one of its dottiest progenies. After the war someone had the idea of setting up an organization to propagate the British way of life throughout the world. This was a godsend for those working within the Ministry of Information. As it began to run down, many of its employees were able to move over to the British Council. From Addis Ababa to Rio de Janeiro, British Council offices sprouted like mushrooms. Those in the Middle East were mostly staffed by some particularly extraordinary people. They spread the good news of the British way of life, by distributing back numbers of *Horizon* and *Country Life* magazines, and lecturing on early Celtic Art or the Religious Significance of Stonehenge to the Druids.

I cannot now recollect how it happened, but shortly after my decision not to join the Press Association, I found myself walking into Lord and Lady Astor's former London residence in St James's Square, to be interviewed for a job with the Film Division of the Ministry of Information or it may have been with the British Council. Vaguely I recollect that it was John Lehmann, no doubt concerned about the state of my health and worried for my future who had had the kindness to recommend me.

When I had shaken the limp hand of Mr Roberts, I knew at once it had been a mistake on my part to have worn my army uniform. The sight of it positively unsettled him.

"Oh dear me," he said. "I'm afraid you've been in the army and can't possibly be suited for this kind of work."

"I could try. Anyway, what is it?"

"Well I suppose, yes I suppose if I had to sum up the ramifications of my department in one word I would use the word RE-EDUCATION, yes RE-EDUCATION would be the *mot juste*."

"Would it be, now?" I commented. "And whom are you re-educating?"

"The Germans, of course."

"With films?"

"That is so," said Mr Roberts. "And you have no knowledge of films, have you?"

"What do you mean by knowledge?"

"Experience in the medium for educational purposes."

"Not exactly. But my favourite film is *Gone with the Wind*." And hoping to impress Mr Roberts with my contacts, I added: "And Vivien Leigh is a personal friend of mine."

"I'm told she leads that poor husband of hers a pretty dance," said Mr Roberts giving me the impression that I would have to know smarter people than Vivien Leigh if I was going to stand a chance of being employed by his Film Division.

The interview seemed to be grinding to a halt so, in order to resuscitate it, I said: "I suppose you're making films of the concentration camps compulsory weekly viewing for the Nazis."

"We've tried that, but it didn't work. They're so horrible that the Germans don't believe them, and think that they've been faked."

"So what kind of films do you show the Nazis?" I asked.

"Films about the British way of life."

"Oh yes, I get it. Early Celtic Art and Cottage Industries," I suggested.

Mr Roberts brightened visibly. "Absolutely. How clever of you to put your finger on it. Perhaps after all you could be of assistance to my department. Oh, by the way we have to carry out all the menial tasks ourselves, like packing and dispatching the films."

"You can stick your fucking films right up your arse," I said.

"Oh dear me," said Mr Roberts and blinked. "Oh dear me. How very rude of you."

"I'm sorry," I said. "It's just that I can't stand Germans and don't think they're worth re-educating. The best thing would be to follow their own policies and exterminate the lot."

To this day I have never altered my opinion of the Germans as being the menace in Europe, even greater than the Russians. I never go to Germany, and never buy anything of German origin if I can avoid doing so. People who buy German cars annoy me, in the same way as do people who buy Japanese. I can never forgive a race who used their captives for bayonet practice and prisoners of war as live targets. I have been accused of being un-Christian in my attitude. But when ever did I claim to be a Christian?

So ended my second attempt to obtain useful employment. But I still had money in the bank, so I decided to live for pleasure as long as it lasted. This has been my policy ever since. Avoid work until the situation becomes desperate, when I am forced to find some kind of job. Only a couple of years ago I was compelled to take employment as general shop labourer in a factory. My tasks included cleaning out the lavatories, sweeping the factory floor, and driving the van. I did not mind the lavatories or the driving, but sweeping that factory floor was soul destroying. It was a machine tool factory and I had to collect the swarf in buckets and cart it outside to a large container. There is something depressing about swarf and I can never look another piece in the eye. But ten months in that factory taught me that I have had a wonderful life compared with the majority of people. I will never blame any factory worker for going on strike no matter how trivial the cause. Factories are the curse of the human race, devitalizing, obscene and dehumanizing.

My circle of acquaintances at the Salisbury pub continued to widen along with the cost of a round of drinks. I became what is known as an easy touch, and every morning in that October of 1946 there was a crowd of mumpers anxiously awaiting my arrival. I did not care. As long as I had the money, I was happy to buy their company if not their friendship. A double whiskey was only three shillings. Sometimes one or two would be waiting outside the pub for me to arrive at eleven in the morning to ask me for a loan. This in the drinking world is known as entrance money. It is strictly non-repayable as the people asking for it are down on their luck. What they want is sufficient coppers to get into the pub and buy half a pint of the cheapest beer. This they will make last until they are able to edge in on a group of drinkers who will start including them in the round. They will not be able to stand their round and if there is any danger of this being demanded, they will slide off and join the fringe of another band of wealthy drinkers. I never begrudge anyone entrance money, nor do I expect down and outs to pay for a round. Those that have the money buy the booze.

Michael and Kevin were two resting actors. I had bought them the odd drink for which, being Irish, they had an unquenchable thirst. But their first love was gambling. I felt sorry for them because however much time they spent studying the form in the morning, whichever horse they chose, the wretched thing invariably ended up at the tail of the field in the afternoon. This they attributed to a number of dishonourable persons, intent on depriving them of their rightful winnings. Either the owner, the trainer, or the jockey, or the horse was bent. Sometimes all four.

In those days betting shops did not exist. Bets were written out on slips of paper and collected by the bookies' runners who worked on commission. This was illegal. The only legal way of betting off the course was to have a credit account with a bookmaker and pass your bets to him by telephone or post. This made betting extremely difficult for the majority of the population, so everyone ignored the law. Bookmakers, however illegal, flourished. The police turned a blind eye in return for payola and only intervened in the event of violent disputes between bookmakers, usually disputes over territory.

On Fridays Michael and Kevin walked to the Westminster Labour Exchange and drew the dole. By closing time, this had passed in to the rapacious hands of Billy the Kid.

Billy the Kid was the stupidest bookmaker I have met, and I have known a great number. The trouble with Billy the Kid was that he began to look upon Michael and Kevin as a sure source of weekly income. In his simple way he concluded that the state would keep on paying them out weekly every Friday, and that by after racing at the latest the money would have found its way into his satchel. So Billy decided to give Michael and Kevin credit. Now a bookmaker should only give credit to credit-worthy clients and never to out of work actors, even if they are on the dole. Admittedly he did not hand out much credit, but by the end of October the sum owing to him had risen to twenty-five pounds.

Michael and Kevin began to look worried, and one day when I arrived at the Salisbury at opening time they were outside waiting for me, and suggested that we give the Salisbury a miss and go across the road to the Green Man for a drink.

After I had bought a round of drinks they came to the point. Would I lend them twenty-five pounds? Billy was pressing them for payment, and although legally there was nothing he could do about it, he was pestering them whenever they went into the Salisbury for a quiet drink.

To their surprise I agreed, on the condition that I gave the money to Billy myself. They were disappointed at this, but under the circumstances they saw it was the best deal available. I often wondered afterwards why I was so easily parted from my money. I can only conclude it was my feeling of insecurity, of my desire to be liked. I was in need of friendship and it seemed to me at the time that it was cheap at the price of twenty-five pounds.

In due course I paid Billy, warning him that if he gave Michael and Kevin further credit, he could not rely on me to act as their banker a second time. I had not the slightest doubt that they would give my name as an impeccable reference. Billy ignored my advice. I heard a few months later that he had gone bust, and he died not long afterwards. Kevin, I never saw again.

At about the same time as my encounter with Michael and Kevin, I met Reg Willis, who was the chief sub. on the *Evening News*. Later on, when he was to become its Editor, he was very kind to me. In the fifties I started writing short stories for his paper, and in the sixties I wrote a weekly column, naturally called Nelson's Column. This was a successful column. Roughly what I tried to do was to write for both men and women, but with the accent on the latter. I would always take women's part against men, so I am proud to say that I was among the advance guard of women's lib and women's rights. Unfortunately the day came for Reg to retire, and some whizz kids moved into his seat, and I went out in a matter of weeks.

One evening at the Salisbury Reg introduced me to Raymond Mould, the heaviest gin drinker I have ever met. Raymond was wearing an old R.A.F. Officer's overcoat. He was balding, and in a fairly high state of drunkenness so that his glasses had slipped down onto the end of his nose. He was not a very pretty sight. His speech was slurred and what he said was very difficult to understand, and his words tumbled over each other in a high-pitched whine.

As I myself began to drink more and more, communications between us became difficult. But I did make out that he was a Press publicist for a number of theatre managements.

"He's the greatest in the game. Got all the best business in London," Reg informed me.

I looked at Raymond who was attempting to add water from a jug to his gin, but missing the glass so that the water splashed across the bar, and found this difficult to believe.

"Fuck," said Raymond. He turned to Reg. "Fucking sodding liars."

"Here we go," said Reg.

"One hundred and sixty-six planes shot down, fuck my arse!"

shouted Raymond. Waving his glass in the air he addressed the drinkers who had gathered round him. "So you thought the brave boys in blue shot down one hundred and sixty-six sodding German planes, didn't you? Sixty-six would be nearer the mark." He wagged his glass at his listeners.

Having delivered himself of this information he lost interest in his theme and turned to Reg and myself and said: "Come on, let's have some more gin."

He felt around in the pocket of his overcoat and pulled out a handful of crumpled notes which he tossed on the bar. Over the next few months I was to see this performance repeated many times.

During the war Raymond had worked at the Air Ministry as an Information Officer. He was referring to a day during the Battle of Britain when the Air Ministry claimed that one hundred and sixty-six German aircraft had been shot down. Raymond knew that this figure was grossly inflated. For some reason it irritated him. He could not see that whether it was true or not was unimportant. I was in England at the time, and can clearly recollect how my own morale was boosted by the claim. I felt for the first time that all was not lost, that the horrible Hun might not be able to cross the Channel.

During the following months I had some nasty moments with Raymond when he started to harangue whoever might be standing next to him in a bar about Churchill's lying habits. Although Churchill had lost the peace, most people including many of those who had voted him out of power at the General Election, felt that he had won the war. The atmosphere could turn nasty, and Raymond was frequently threatened with violence. Like most drunkards he was unaware of the danger into which his antipathy towards Churchill was placing him and always reluctant to be moved. I found the best way was to tell him there was no more gin in the particular bar. This had the effect of sending him lurching towards the door, where he would turn and spit out his parting shot to the infuriated company: "One hundred and sixty-six fucking planes, my fucking arse."

Subsequently what Raymond was saying in 1946 was admitted to be the truth. But at the time I prayed that he would keep quiet. If he had been attacked I am afraid he would have been severely damaged. I have never seen fit to lay down my life for my friends.

On the first night I met Raymond, when the Salisbury closed, together with Reg Willis we made our way to Manzi's Restaurant in Leicester Street. I had known this seafood restaurant before the war, and it never lost its high standard and its amazing value for money.

While Reg and I moved on from spirits to lager, Raymond stuck to his gin. Reg happened to mention some actress who had recently died. This carelessness on Reg's part was too much for Raymond, who began to weep copious tears. They poured down his cheeks into his glass.

Not liking to see good gin go to waste I suggested that he drink it up. Raymond smiled at me through his tears and said: "I like you, Michael. You're a wonderful person. Come and see me tomorrow."

"Where and what time?"

"What is time?" said Raymond. "What is fucking time but the sodding death cell in which we are all incarcerated."

At least that's roughly what he said, but it took him some minutes to get the words out, and "incarcerated" caused him much trouble.

Sometimes I used to go to the Coffee Inn in Leicester Square if I had arrived before eleven when the Salisbury opened.

"Eleven o'clock. The Coffee Inn," I suggested.

Soon afterwards Raymond threw another bunch of crumpled notes onto the table. When the waiter brought the change he stuffed it into his pocket without counting it, leaving a pound tip on the table. As we walked away I saw that Raymond had not touched the food he had ordered.

The next morning I went to the Coffee Inn but not to meet Raymond. I had forgotten all about our arrangement but it was ten minutes before opening time.

"Good morning, Michael."

I looked up and recognized Raymond. He was very pale, and would have been even whiter had there not been a night's growth of dark stubble on his chin.

He slouched down opposite me, and I ordered him a coffee.

"It was good fun last night," I said by way of getting the conversation going.

Raymond shook his head but did not say a word.

A waitress placed a cup of hot coffee in front of him. Its aroma proved too much for Raymond who pushed it away with a shaking hand.

"You don't look at all well," I said.

Raymond nodded, opened his mouth as if about to speak, but the effort proved too much for him.

Noticing for the first time the soiled condition of his R.A.F. overcoat, I said: "You ought to get that cleaned."

Raymond stared at me. I began to feel that I was not communicating.

I gave up the effort of bridging the gap and sipped my coffee, noticing that my hand was shaking violently. Suddenly Raymond lurched to his feet, and rushed towards the door. I did not care if I never saw the man again, but I was intrigued at his behaviour. To begin with I thought he had been taken short and was off to the lavatory either to crap or to vomit. Instead he made his way into the street, with me in close pursuit.

At the first pub he brushed past the man who was opening the doors, staggered to the bar and ordered two large gins. As the first one was placed on the bar he seized it with both hands and drank it neat and the second was dealt with in similar fashion.

For the first time he spoke: "How I detest gin."

I considered this a strange remark considering that from what I had seen of him he probably bathed in the stuff.

"Forgive me," he said. "What would you like? A whiskey."

I noticed that Raymond ordered a large one for me, and in all the time I knew him I never saw him drink a single.

I added a good measure of water to my Scotch.

"That's what I like about you, that's why you're a wonderful person. You only drink water with your Scotch."

It seemed to me an odd measure by which anyone should be judged, but before I could say anything Raymond continued: "I want you to come and work for me."

In spite of what Reg had said about Raymond, declaring him to be the best theatre publicist in the business, my immediate reaction was one of doubt. I had seen many drunks in my time, was one myself, but Raymond's capacity for gin seemed to me to be excessive. On the other hand my search for employment had not so far been successful, so working on the principle that I had nothing to lose I asked him what kind of a job he had in mind. I was not even sure what a theatre publicist had to do.

"Just get the fucking public to come to some fucking awful shows," said Raymond in answer to my question. "Take a few journalists out and feed them up with stories about the actors and actresses, none of which is fucking true. I've got a fund of silly stories you can use over and over again. You know the kind of fucking thing. 'While playwright Michael Nelson was storming the monastery at Cassino an old copy of *The Times* blew into his fucking trench, and he saw that leading actress Nora Titsoff had just had a baby. If I come through this lot, swore Michael Nelson to himself, I will write a play called *The Cunts of Cassino* and Nora Titsoff will play the lead. Unfortunately Michael Nelson did fucking well come through, and tonight's unlucky first nighters will have to sit through three interminably boring acts of *The Cunts of Cassino.*' " Raymond paused for breath and for the first time smiled sadly. "You could write that kind of crap, couldn't you? After all you did say last night that you had worked for Cudlipp on the *Sunday Pic*."

"I could have a go," I said.

"Then there are the first night Press bars. All you have to do is to get the critics so pissed they don't know what utter rubbish they're watching, and they go away and write good notices. At least that's the theory. Sometimes the booze makes them so irritable that they go and write something bloody awful, although they've never seen one single act of the play because they've been too stoned out of their tiny minds. Anyway, let's go and get a drink somewhere else. I hate this place."

Raymond was an itinerant drinker. He could never stay in a bar for more than ten minutes. I don't know what he was looking for. Probably someone to love. When I got to know him better, first of all I thought he was queer, but later on I came to the conclusion that he was sexless. This may have accounted for his unreasonable hatred for certain people. But beneath his malice and bitterness, he had an intense love for the theatre. What is more he had a vast knowledge of it and knew everyone who was connected with it from important managements, from what he called "the silly fuckers who think they're sodding stars," down to the humblest spear carrier. In spite of his outbursts of unreasonable rage, with few exceptions everybody loved him, as I was to discover in due course.

As we drifted round the bars that morning and Raymond became more and more intoxicated I learned something of his background. He had been born near Nottingham and had eventually worked on the *Nottingham Post*, and from there had specialized in show business, or Miss Tinseltwot as he referred to it, and eventually came to Fleet Street. He had served through the war as an Information

Officer in the R.A.F. and was now working for a firm of theatre publicists called Vivian, Ellis, and Mould. But as far as I could make out it consisted solely of Mould. It appeared that Ellis had gone off to set up his own company.

When I asked who Vivian was, Raymond said: "Tony Vivian. Lord Vivian. You must meet him as soon as possible. I'll ring him up and ask him to invite us down for the week-end. He's about to go into partnership with C.B."

In the course of further alcoholic conversation I gathered Raymond really did have a large number of clients among whom were C. B. Cochran, Henry Sherek, Linnit and Dunfee and numerous other London and provincial managements. He was also supposed to look after the personal publicity of several leading actors and actresses. I do not think they benefited greatly from Raymond's care, because every time they asked him what he was doing to promote their interests he regarded their reasonable enquiries as gross impertinence. "Who the hell do they think they are, demanding my personal attention?" he would shout. "Bloody actors. Just a bunch of prima donnas."

These outbursts would occasionally lose Raymond a client, but for an unfathomable reason the majority stayed with him. Actors and actresses must be natural masochists.

I cannot remember where Raymond and I parted company that day. It may have been at the Salisbury before closing time, or it may have been at Manzi's. But I do remember going to the downstairs bar at the Embassy Club and mauling the Yorkshire hostess and begging her to let me go to bed with her.

I woke the following morning with a splitting head and staggered to the basin to slake my thirst. As I crossed the room I saw a letter had been pushed under the door. I opened it with difficulty. It was from my father asking me to lunch at the L'Aperitif, after which he proposed that we should proceed to the city where he had made arrangements for me to sign the necessary documents relating to my trust. I looked at the date and cursed aloud as I realized that it was that very morning he was expecting me. The letter must have been delivered the previous day, and I had failed to notice it after coming home from the Embassy in the early hours. Luckily, however much I drank in those days I always woke early. This was a result of my army training, and an inborn fear of being late for the morning parade which could result in unpleasantness. I immediately telephoned my father and confirmed that I would meet him at one o'clock at the restaurant, and faced the problem of making myself presentable.

My uniform lay in a crumpled heap on the floor, and to wear it was out of the question. Examination of my face in the mirror revealed bloodshot eyes, purple face made even more hideous by a heavy growth of stubble. My hands were shaking so violently that there was no question of shaving myself. It was eight o'clock. I tottered down the stairs, passing a few tarts on the way. They were indefatigable and offered a twenty-four-hour service. I went out into the street, and called in at the chemists and threw back their number one pick-up, known as kill or cure. The way I felt that morning I would preferred to have died. A few minutes later I was in the hot room of the Turkish bath, gasping for breath as the booze and grime began to ooze from my pores.

The Jermyn Street Turkish baths were fantastic value. Just after the war they cost about ten shillings a night. For this you could sweat it out, swim in the pool, have a massage for which one paid a little extra, and roll up in a thick bath towel and sleep through the night until one was called the next morning by an attendant with a cup of coffee.

At midday I emerged from the baths still shaking and feeling weak at the knees. For one moment I felt inclined to leave a message at the L'Aperitif which was also in Jermyn Street, that I had been stricken down with a sudden onslaught of 'flu. But the thought of finally getting my hands on my trust money won the day, and I went into the barber's and asked for a shave and face massage.

My grandfather who had died in the late twenties had been a successful business man, and had set up a trust fund for each of his grandchildren. The income from these trusts was used for our education, and at the age of twenty-one the income came to us. I had been overseas when I came of age, and my father had decided that nothing could be done until I returned to England. But I knew through my eldest brother who had come of age before the war that the income would be somewhere between two hundred and two hundred and fifty pounds a year.

I was late arriving at the L'Aperitif and found my father and my step-mother Jane already seated at the table.

"What would you like to drink?" asked my father.

"Whiskey, please."

When the drink was placed before me I was presented with a considerable problem. How could I convey it with my shaking hands to my mouth without spilling it over the table cloth? I counted three, seized it with both hands, and got it to my mouth in one movement. The glass hit my teeth and its contents splashed into my mouth. For one moment I feared I might spit them out on the table, but with supreme self-control I held and swallowed them.

Jane, who was next to me, winked at me and said: "You need another."

I consider this to have been a most civilized remark. She claims to this day that she has never seen anyone in her whole life who looked so ghastly as I did that morning.

The meal was a nightmare. I do not know if the food was good or bad except I can remember my father poking at a bit of meat and saying: "Bloody horsemeat."

This was probably true. A considerable amount of that delicacy was served in those days under various guises. Very good it was too. Only the English disapprove of it because the English ruling classes love their horses more than they do their children.

Jane continued to ply me with whiskey and I did my best to swallow a few mouthfuls of the horsemeat without regurgitating it, no mean achievement on my part.

Finally that awful meal drew to its close. I said good-bye to Jane who was off to Harrods to do some shopping, and set off with my father to the City.

The solicitor's office was small and dusty. I was introduced to a man who informed me that he was representing my interests, and invited me to sit down in a high backed chair. No sooner had I done so than I was overcome by drowsiness. The late night and the lunch time booze had caught up with me.

My father seated himself on my right. The solicitor picked up a piece of parchment which looked like the original Magna Carta and started to read.

The sound of his voice droning on was too much for me and I fell asleep. I was rudely awakened by a loud voice: "Mr Nelson, you must not go to sleep at a time like this."

I opened my eyes and saw the shocked look on the face of my solicitor, I apologized and he returned to his task of enumerating the clauses in Magna Carta.

When he had finished he asked: "Now are you aware of what your rights are?"

I had no idea what they were. All I could think of was my bed and a long sleep.

"Yes," I said.

"Let me repeat then, that the monies in this trust are yours absolutely if you so wish. But if you wish otherwise it is within your power to appoint the bank and your father as co-trustees."

Only later on was I to appreciate what he was talking about. In simple language it meant that the capital of the trust, some £8,000, was mine to do with it as I wished, blow the lot if I cared, or I could appoint my father and the bank as my trustees thereby losing my right to the capital and only receiving the income. There were other clauses in the trust. If I chose the latter course I could draw so much of the capital towards buying a house or setting up a business, but only with the permission of the trustees.

Like a fool I signed my capital away that day. I appointed my father and the bank as co-trustees. In the years ahead this was to cause considerable friction between myself and my father. For two years we did not speak or meet one another, because he refused to release capital from my trust for the purpose of buying a house. He argued that I had no steady job, and a job must come before a house. He was entitled to his opinion, but I thought and still think he was wrong.

There are two lessons to be learned from that day I signed my rights away. The first is that fathers should never try to hang on to the right to administer their children's money when they come of age. If their children want to ride to the devil with it, that's their affair. The second lesson, and far more important, is never to sign any kind of document under the influence of drink; always read the small print, and be absolutely sure what you are signing.

I did in fact have considerable difficulty in signing Magna Carta. When the solicitor handed me a pen, my hand was shaking so badly, that I had to clutch it with both hands in order to make my mark. But that scrawl on the document signed away my birthright.

As I left the office I noticed that the solicitor looked shocked. He must have thought I had behaved in a frivolous manner. He probably did not realize that I was as drunk as a lord.

Anyway, I could now look forward to a private income of about five pounds a week which must be at least the equivalent of thirty pounds today. So I was a lucky young man.

I was becoming more and more disenchanted with my flat in Jermyn Street. The noise at night was becoming intolerable. The building shook as bodies bumped and ground. In addition, the flat was becoming very cold. It had only been roughly repaired from the ravages of a bomb, and draughts howled in from all directions. The weather grew colder and colder, and to make matters worse the electricity supply was constantly being cut off at the power stations. The winter of 1946 was to be the coldest that Britain had experienced this century.

The decision to move was taken out of my hands when I received notice from the landlords to quit. One or two of the girls on my landing were pretty sore about this, but pointed out that I was hardly in a position to pay an economical rent for a room in a brothel. But I thought one of them was being a bit brutal when she said to me: "It's not as if you've got anything to sell, have you ducks? I mean no one could exactly call you a beauty."

So I began a trek round the offices of the Estate Agents. I was horrified at the shortage of rented accommodation in London, and at the price asked for the humblest of rooms. Before the war I had paid thirty shillings a week for a large room in a house in Bloomsbury, next door to Virginia and Leonard Woolf. And that included breakfast.

The estate agents were having a bonanza. They could sell or let anything on their books. Not only did they not care a damn, but they made no effort to conceal their indifference to my plight. I began to see what they meant about homes fit for heroes.

I had of course mentioned my problem to my friend David Kentish. One day in the Salisbury, forty-eight hours before I was due to be evicted from my brothel, he told me that an actor friend of his was off to America and wanted someone to take over his flat in his absence abroad. It was not cheap, and would cost me eighty pounds a month. I immediately accepted the offer, especially when I heard that the flat had central heating and that hot water came out of the taps at unspecified hours.

The flat was in Dolphin Square and consisted of two rooms, a small kitchen and a bathroom. The furniture was hideous and broken down. There was one saucepan and a kettle without a lid in the kitchen. But it was at least a refuge. The rent was scandalously high, and David explained to me that the original lease was held by a money-grabbing lady who paid £80 a year for the flat, which included the rates. So by letting it furnished to David's actor friend she was able to make a handsome profit.

I have always thought since that day that there must be something to be said for taking living accommodation out of private hands. Certainly ever since 1946, people's lives have been made miserable by shortage of living accommodation, while the unscrupulous or the clever have grown fat on their discomfort. No party has come anywhere near to solving the housing problem, and today the situation is as bad as it has ever been. Single rooms rent for as much as twenty pounds a week, and flats of two or possibly three bedrooms are let for three figures weekly.

It was shortly after I had moved into the relative warmth and comfort of Dolphin Square that I fell in love.

I had not been in love since my abortive attempt to get off with the Italian Contessa in Udine where we had found ourselves, following the cessation of hostilities. She had led me a pretty dance, while her husband, one of the leading local fascists, had been in hiding. The last time I had seen her she had been kneeling in a bath before my friend Lieutenant Mark of American Intelligence, prepared to do anything to prevent her husband from being shot. There was something degrading about the scene, but it was her eyes that I particularly remembered. Mark had struck her across the face and shouted at her: "Got to work it off haven't you, you bloody little fascist beast. That's right, keep at it and maybe I won't have your old man put up against the wall and shot."

I could remember how she had looked up at him and through the steam I saw no tears in her eyes, only hatred.

She had then turned towards me and there had still been no softening in those eyes.

Although my drivers had never mentioned my disastrous love affair, if that's the word, with the Contessa, I knew they thought I had made a right idiot of myself. Which had been a good reason for not falling in love again. I do not know if you can regulate love in that way. At least one can try. I determined never to get involved with one person. I would go to bed with them, but as soon as a relationship started to rear its head, I vowed that I would draw back and take care.

It never works that way, however much we tell ourselves that we will not get involved.

The object of my love was Julia. I would like to divulge her true name, but now that she is an international star I think that would be unfair. I can only hope that if she reads this, at least it may give her cause for laughter. But I doubt it. She was not blessed with a sense of humour.

David Kentish introduced me to Julia at the Salisbury. She was singing in a review in the West End, and from the first time I met her I could sense that she was an ambitious girl. One had only to look at the way she fawned on Laurence Olivier. I am quite sure she would have dropped her knickers for him had he made the slightest pass at her, which he did not. There was a definite pattern in the way she treated men. It depended entirely on where they ranked in the theatrical world. Leading actors, managers and important directors were honoured with her smiles. The lesser ones might receive a brief glance. People like myself, outside the theatre, were completely ignored.

The trouble was that I was fascinated by her looks. She was tall, slim, blonde, blue eyed, graced with a pair of chorus girl's legs that started somewhere around her waist.

I suspect that I may sound bitchy about Julia, particularly in view of what follows. But she was decidedly dim. Admittedly she had plenty of chatter and gossip about the theatre. She may indeed for all I know have been a good actress. But I had to admit to myself at the time, that my love for her was scarcely on an intellectual plane. In no way did I pretend to myself that it was anything else but love of that body beautiful. But so bewitched was I by her looks that I set about seeing if there was any possible way of seducing her.

After considering my assets from all angles, I had to admit they did not add up to much. I possessed a crumpled uniform, a suit from Harrods, had an income of £250 a year and a thousand pounds in the bank.

I considered the possibilities. I could try the direct approach, the straight "Do you fuck?" whispered in her ear. I have been told that this shock tactic can effect as high as a ten percent success rate. In my case it has produced withdrawal symptoms or a violent reaction with a hand across my face. I did have one success with this method many years ago. "Yes, I do," she said sending my blood pressure way out over the top. "But the trouble is I sometimes think you love me only for my body," she added.

I should have kept my mouth shut. The trouble was that I was stoned out of my mind. Without a thought as to the consequences I replied. "But, my darling, how could I love you for your fucking mind?"

She was a lovely girl. She never spoke to me again. I bitterly regret to this day those careless words uttered years and years ago.

I wondered if my new found friend Raymond Mould might be able to help me. After all he knew everyone who was of any importance in the theatre, and might be able to persuade some impresario to offer her a leading part. But enquiries revealed that Raymond was out of London for several weeks, publicizing one of his plays which was on tour.

On second thoughts too this did not seem such a good idea. If the impresario had the same tastes as I had, he would no doubt wish to subject Julia to the indignities of his casting couch.

As a young man I had written poetry and even managed to have some of it published. There were also my unpublished war poems. But somehow I could not see Julia crouching before the dim electric fire in my new flat in Dolphin Square as I read them aloud. She did not seem the sort of girl who would appreciate cosy evenings at home.

I could have told her that I was a friend of Dylan Thomas. But Dylan was drunk the whole time and not as famous as he was to be after his death, when the whole world was to become his friend. I knew Julia was a snob, and dearly loved a lord, but I hadn't got one in tow. I cursed the day when I had not cultivated the acquaintance of the Princesses Elizabeth and Margaret, whom I frequently met out riding in Windsor Great Park. I used to doff my cap to them, but little did I know at the time that one of them was to be the Queen of England. How different my life might have been if we had exchanged nursery teas with one another.

I was still circling round the object of my love, keeping very much in the background and only speaking to when spoken to (which was very seldom, usually a "Yes, please," when I offered to buy her a drink) when one day I happened to produce my cheque book in the Salisbury to obtain some money from George Holmes.

As a result of signing my trust deed, I now had a personal account with Coutts Bank. In those days Coutts was the smart bank, numbering among its clients, as it still does, the Monarch. As I wrote out the cheque, I noticed for the first time that Julia was actually looking at me.

The following day I could hardly believe my good luck. David Kentish, Julia and a couple of actors had decided to lunch at the Ivy, and at Julia's suggestion I was invited to join the party.

I know I am giving the impression that Julia was a mercenary girl. She probably was. Many years later an antique dealer was to tell me that there is nothing in this world you cannot buy if you have the money. This statement may be offensive to women. I believe it to be only partly true, but would add that if money can buy anything it can buy men as well as women.

The Ivy was the theatrical restaurant, and actors and actresses made up the majority of its clientele. It was as equally prestigious to be seen eating there as at the Savoy Grill. Why it should be prestigious to be seen eating in public at a vogue restaurant is difficult to explain. Maybe it gives an actor or actress a feeling of security, of having arrived. Maybe there is the hope eternal that they will be spotted. Maybe it's the natural egotism of the profession, the necessity to be on show, off the stage as well as on.

Anyway, I could see that the Ivy was Julia's idea of heaven. I reckoned too that my Coutts cheque book had impressed her. Accordingly I laid my plans and bided my time.

Luck was on my side. Without warning the notices went up at Julia's revue, and she found herself out of work. This meant of course that she was free during the evenings, when many of her grand friends were working.

Shortly after her show had closed I came into the Salisbury one evening to find her standing by the bar with a couple of nondescript out-of-work actors keeping her company. I noticed that she was sipping a half of bitter. Julia did not believe in buying herself drinks, and I assumed that the half pint of bitter was all that her companions could afford to stand her.

"Do you know what would be nice?" I said going up to her.

"What?" she said. This was the first word she had addressed to me for several days and I was grateful. The shock of finding herself out of work had rendered her speechless as far as I was concerned.

"A bottle of champagne."

Julia brightened. "That would be fun," she said turning her back on the two resting actors.

I ordered a bottle across the bar from George who brought it up from the cellar and placed it in an ice bucket. He seemed to find the situation amusing, leant across the bar and whispered "You're wasting your money."

I was well aware that I was not the only person at the Salisbury who was after Julia's body. Indeed there may have been some who were in pursuit of her mind. For a moment I thought of abandoning the chase. Was it worth it? What was the point of spending a lot of money, only to be rebuffed in the end? But by the time I had weighed the pros and cons, George had removed the cork from the bottle and the sparkling wine was in the glasses. Looking at Julia as she raised it to her sensual lips was too much for my lust.

"Delicious," she said, putting down the glass and flicking her tongue around her lips, which brought me to a point of ecstasy. I knew I was prepared to spend my last penny on her.

I had to strike while we were still alone, except for the two actors who were mumbling to one another, sulky at having been excluded from the delights of the champagne by Julia. I could hear them murmuring mutinously: "Bitch ... tart ... some people have all the luck."

"Julia," I said. "What about a dozen oysters?"

This was the first time I had used this opening gimmick, and it has stood me in good stead since, particularly as I have grown older. After all one cannot say to a girl: "How much are you going to cost?", not to a nice girl anyway. But a reference to oysters lets them know that you are not the mean sort, that you are not going to count the cost of their company and anything else they may have to offer.

"That would be fun," said Julia.

I could sense that I still had a long way to go with her, but at least she had managed to address four consecutive words to me.

"But let's crack a second bottle first," I said keen to follow up my advantage. "George, what about opening another?"

George Holmes looked stunned. Leaning across the bar he whispered: "Never make it. Keep your money. Not worth it."

"What's that you're mumbling about, George?" asked Julia.

I prayed that she had not caught the gist of George's conversation. I have always believed that if you pray hard enough, your prayers stand a better chance of being granted.

"Giving Michael a tip for the three-thirty tomorrow. But it's an odds on chance," said George winking at me.

I wished he would go away. I felt he could easily foul up the whole situation and set me back in square one.

We finished the first bottle of champagne, and by the time we were half-way down the second, I felt that Julia had begun to acknowledge my existence.

"What do you do, Michael?" she asked. "I've noticed you hanging round this pub for the last few weeks, but that's all."

I did not consider this complimentary but it was a true statement of fact.

"I've just come back from Italy. I've been in the Middle East and Italy for four and a half years."

"How boring," said Julia.

"Yes, it was," I said. "Very, very boring."

There seemed a nasty gap looming in our scintillating conversation: "I'm just finding my feet," I continued.

"Oh, yes," said Julia.

I was becoming desperate. "Yes, I'm going to be a writer, I mean I was a writer before I went away, and I'm going to start all over again."

"Then you can write a play for me," said Julia.

I detected a slight tone of interest in her voice. Subsequently I was to discover that mention you are a writer to an actor or an actress and they will do one of two things. Ask you to write a play for them if they are successful, or ask you to write a part in a play for them, if they are not.

"I have one in mind. There is a super part in it for you," I said.

This was a lie and rash of me for she immediately said: "Tell me about it."

I countered by saying: "No, I don't want to spoil it. But I would like you to read it when it's finished. I would hate you to see it in its rough state, as it might put you off."

Three-quarters of an hour later we had finished the second bottle and left the muttering actors behind. As we went to the door George came out from behind the bar shook me by the hand and wished me the best of luck.

When we were in the taxi Julia said: "What does George find so funny?"

"He's a very old friend of mine. We fought together in the desert," I lied, wondering if tales of heroism, which I would have no great difficulty in fabricating, would impress her.

"How boring ... I mean the desert."

"Very flat, like Norfolk," I said hoping that she would appreciate that I had read my Coward.

Either she did not hear me, or she did not appreciate my knowledge of the so-called Master, for she said: "Where are we going?"

"Wheelers, if that's all right with you."

"Oh," she said.

I had the impression that Wheelers was not her idea of the sort of place where she should be seen. Perhaps it was the Ivy or nothing. Sensing that I had put a foot wrong I added: "Then we'll go on and dine at the Ivy."

Julia brightened visibly. She had been sitting in the corner of the taxi as far away from me as possible. I may have been wrong, but it seemed to me that she moved at least half an inch closer to me.

I have always loved Wheelers ever since I first went there. Its owner Bernard Walsh has always understood the financial problems facing writers, artists, and gamblers (being an owner of horses himself). Wheelers staff may change with the passing of time but they always appreciate a pretty girl. I like to think that they have all been my friends. Unfortunately eating at Wheelers has become somewhat more expensive over the last few years, and I no longer pop in there as frequently for a plate of fish and chips. Indeed only recently I put my head round the door to say hello to the staff. They were panic stricken imagining that I proposed to eat there. "You can't afford to eat here," one of them said to me, and proceeded to take me to a pub in Old Compton Street and buy me a drink.

I still love Wheelers and of course it's no more expensive to eat there than anywhere else.

Julia was a great success that evening. By the time we had eaten a dozen oysters sitting at the bar, she had begun to loosen up and talk to me.

Nevertheless I knew that she was anxious to get to the Ivy. So having bid good-night to my friends at Wheelers, we took a taxi for the two hundred yards or so that separated us from the Ivy.

On arrival at the Ivy I quickly tracked down the head waiter while Julia was attending to her face, and with my usual sleight of hand passed him one of the old white five pound notes, whispering to him that I wished to sit at a table where my guest would be in full view.

I cannot say that I really enjoyed that dinner. But I kept telling myself that it was just another brick in the bridge I was building to Julia's heart. To begin with Julia preened herself like an oriental bird, waving her hands in all directions, and occasionally blowing kisses. I was hard put to keep my temper when various men came to our table to kiss her on both cheeks telling her how marvellous she had been in her revue, and consoling her because it had closed. Julia made no effort to introduce me to them. I knew that she felt that I was not worthy of her.

I kept reminding myself to be patient, to remember that I was playing for high stakes with few assets. All I had was a Coutts cheque book, and a few pounds in the bank.

It must have been towards midnight when we left the Ivy. I had suggested going on to the Embassy for a final drink.

"No thank you. I must get my sleep in. It's so important for us actresses, you know," she said.

I put her in a taxi outside the restaurant.

"Where do you want to be taken?" I asked.

"I'll tell him," said Julia.

"How much will it cost?" I asked, determined to behave like a gentleman to the bitter end.

"Give me a pound," said Julia.

I handed her the note. The taxi drove away.

I found myself standing alone on the curb outside the Ivy. I felt sad. Julia had not even taken the trouble to say good night, let alone to thank me for the evening.

When the next taxi came by I stopped it, and told the driver to take me to the Embassy. Downstairs in the bar I proceeded to drink whiskey after whiskey. I was not even interested in the Yorkshire tart, nor did I feel like listening to the nostalgic tunes that the pianist was playing. All I could see was Julia's face.

That was the beginning of my big spending spree.

# 7

There is nothing more pathetic than a man in love being taken for a ride by a beautiful girl.

Which is what Julia proceeded to do with me.

She really should have gone into business in the city where she could have employed her talents as an asset stripper to the full. But in her defence I must say that she never gave me any cause for jealousy. Although I doubt if she had the slightest affection for me, and I certainly knew that I held no sexual attraction for her, while she was working on me she did not put it about elsewhere, as the expression goes. Perhaps she sensed that I would not stand for that. She was clever enough to know that as long as I believed that one day she might succumb to my lust, just so long would she be able to manipulate me. In other words while I still had hope, I remained a potential gold mine whose seams she could exploit.

I seem to be making Julia out to be a right bitch. I did not think that at the time. It's only in retrospect that I can see that she used me abominably. I do not hold it against her. She taught me a lesson which was to stand me in good stead in the perilous years that lay ahead.

A few days after we had dined together at the Ivy I was in the Salisbury at my usual hour doing my best to drown my hangover with a bottle of champagne.

"That little tart will ruin you," said George Holmes after I had related the events of my evening out with Julia. "You know how much this stuff is costing you?" he added, pointing to the bottle of Veuve Cliquot. "Fifteen quid a bottle. Mind you it's genuine. But it still won't persuade her to go to bed with you."

"Whoever talked about bed?" I said. "Why does everything in your mind have to relate to sex?"

George roared with laughter. "You have got it fucking bad. You poor old sod. Look, I'll lay you ten to one that you never fuck her."

"How delicately you express yourself," I said. "Nevertheless, you're on. Make it five pounds to fifty."

"You're on your honour to tell the truth," said George. "No saying you've had it away with her when you haven't so much as put your hand on her pussy."

I winced at George's vulgarity.

At that moment Julia came in through the St Martin's Lane door. I was agreeably surprised to notice that as soon as she caught sight of me she immediately made her way towards me.

"A glass of champagne?" I suggested as soon as she had reached me.

"Michael, I've got a cab outside. Would you be an angel and pay it off for me?"

"Of course. Here, help yourself to a drink."

I hurried outside, paid off the taxi and returned in high spirits at having been able to oblige Julia, if only in a humble capacity.

There was one good thing about Julia. As I got to know her better I never had to make conversation. I have never known anyone, not even another actor or actress, so able to sustain such an unceasing flow of chatter about herself. She could range over the course of her twenty years, from her pre-natal existence to her immediate prospects of seeing her name in lights, not just in Shaftesbury Avenue, but in every capital in the world.

Until that morning, she had taken little notice of me. But as soon as she had decided that I was to be her constant escort and companion, which she must have determined the previous evening or during the course of her beauty sleep, I became the receptacle for her thoughts. These had no logical sequence. She would dart from one subject to another with amazing speed. I was continually fascinated by the disconnected flow of her words.

Julia's conversation would go something like this. "Yes, Michael, I will get on to my agent today. Mind you he's absolutely useless. But then all agents are useless until you've made a name for yourself." Here she would put forward her pretty chin and purse her lips. "And I'm bloody well going to the top. Are you listening, Michael? Which reminds me I must visit my osteopath this afternoon. Mummy should never have allowed me to ride a pony. They're madly dangerous and might have ruined my career. Remind me to show you the X-rays of my spine. You'll adore them. And don't forget I've got a session with John Vickers. I'm sure he's the best photographer at the moment. Or do you think I should go to Baron? What did Larry say to you about me? I'm sure he admires my work and is going to offer me something. The trouble with the English theatre today is that they don't appreciate talent. It's quite different in Russia. That's where artists like myself are properly looked after. I mean it's a disgrace that someone like me with my talent should be out of work. I feel ever so hungry but I must watch my figure. I put on three and a half ounces last week. Isn't that too terrible for words? Now where are we going to eat? I would like to go to the Savoy Grill, but be sure that beastly Luigi gives us a table in the center where I can be seen. I think it was quite wrong of him to put me in the corner last time, and frankly I think you should have told him off. But the trouble with you, Michael, is that you won't fight. You're much too soft and easily put off. You ought to try to be more like me and stand up for yourself."

Luigi was the famous *maître d'hôtel*, with a keen eye for the ladies, and an expert at "dressing" the grill room with them. I was to be his friend for many years until I made the stupid mistake of interfering with his "placement" not realizing that to him it was an art. Long after Julia had gone out of my life, I went to the grill room wearing a dinner jacket. As I was waiting by the door I was approached by an American: "Hi, waiter," he called at me. "A table for four."

I must have been drunk. Nothing else can explain my action. Without hesitation I held my arm in the air, and conducted the American and his party across the grill room, until I came to a vacant table. I swept back the chairs and ushered the ladies into their seats.

"That's great," said the American proffering me a five pound note which I palmed, thinking how good it was to be on the receiving end for a change.

Feeling very pleased with myself I made my way back to Luigi's desk by the door. I had no intention of robbing him. I held out the five pound note. As he took it, I could see that he was really angry.

"You will never eat here again," he said, turning his back on me to greet a new party that had just come in.

I never did. Not as long as the great Luigi ruled the Grill Room.

Although the weather outside was growing colder and colder, as November gave way to December in that winter of 1946, I was warm enough in the sunshine of Julia's company. For the first time since I had arrived home I felt happy; I had a purpose in life. That purpose was to please Julia. The whole pattern of my life changed. I no longer frequented the Salisbury. One day Julia had pronounced it boring and filled with boring people. She pointed out that places like the Rivoli bar at the Ritz, the upstairs bars at the Savoy or the Café Royal, were far more comfortable and free of riff-raff.

Julia took great care of her figure. She would only eat with me once a day. According to her mood she would grant me the pleasure of her company for either lunch or dinner. I will say in her favour too that she was seldom late, and if she ever kept me waiting it was because she had been to see someone in pursuit of her career. She never let me doubt for one moment that her career came first, and I am happy for her that her perseverance against all the odds was eventually to take her to the top. I like to think of the immense pleasure that seeing her name in lights must afford her.

There was hardly a posh hotel that we did not visit for lunch or dinner. While I greatly favoured the old Berkeley Hotel, Julia still preferred the Ivy. She quite liked the restaurant overlooking the park at the Ritz, to me the most beautiful place to eat in the world. But the trouble was, as she never ceased to point out, "It's not a place where people would go to look at me."

When I say my purpose in life was to please Julia, I must make it clear that this was not altruism on my part. I wanted to please her, because I believed that was the only way I could persuade her to share my bed. And when I say I was happy, I was only happy in the sense that I was determined to experience this wonderful event. In fact I was in considerable discomfort the whole time I was with Julia as I was in a permanent state of sexual excitement.

At the back of my mind I knew that the situation could not continue. There was first of all the financial aspect to be considered. Almost daily I found myself walking into Coutts & Co. in the Strand to cash a cheque for twenty pounds. With nothing coming in, except for my small private income, it was clear even to me that something would have to be done.

When I was not with Julia I spent most of my time lying on my bed in my flat in Dolphin Square, thinking about her. Over and over again I considered the advantages and the disadvantages of the direct approach method. I had no intention of putting it crudely or using any Anglo-Saxon words. On the other hand, I could not wait for ever. I had to face the fact that as soon as my cash ran out Julia would start looking for another source of income. It took me a lot of courage, but once I had forced myself to acknowledge the facts of the case I knew I would have to go ahead and take some positive action.

It turned out to be easier than I had anticipated.

I was sitting with Julia in the cocktail bar at the Savoy one morning when Julia let out a snort.

"Just look at that couple over there, Michael. I think it's absolutely disgusting. People shouldn't smooch together in public. It's too embarrassing for words. If you tried that sort of thing I should get up and leave."

As I had felt all that morning like leaping on Julia, let alone holding her hand, I thought it wiser to keep quiet.

"Well, what have you to say?" she demanded aggressively.

"Julia, my darling," I said. "You might as well know I'm in love with you. I've been in love with you from the day you had your first glass of champagne with me."

"What has that to do with it?"

"You had better know the truth," I said. "If I can't go to bed with you soon I shall jump into the Thames."

"It would be very cold."

I think my protestation had not been expected. I had noticed in the past that when she was taken by surprise, it took her several seconds to assess the situation before returning her verdict.

Her answer when it came was not very satisfactory. "A great many men love me, Michael," she said. She picked up her glass and sipped her champagne. "But in my opinion a physical relation spoils everything."

"How do you mean spoils...?"

"Let me finish," she said. "What I mean is that if I gave myself to you like a common tart I would have no respect either for you or myself."

I nearly gasped aloud to hear this old bromide trotted out.

"First of all I don't see what a tart has to do with it. Secondly if I love you and you love me, surely sex would be super and lack of respect wouldn't enter into it."

"You must be extremely dense if you cannot understand what I am saying. Most people are able to, or are you saying I'm incapable of expressing myself clearly?"

"All I'm saying is that I don't see what a tart..."

"I've no doubt at all that you find them more amusing than me. I assume that you're one of those squalid little men who think nothing of picking up a girl to satisfy their lust..."

The situation was getting out of control.

"I refuse to quarrel with you," I said.

"Who's talking about quarrelling? Can't I have a straight conversation with you, without you accusing me of trying to pick a quarrel?"

"I'm sorry I started this conversation," I said. "But you might as well know the truth. I'm sexually attracted by you. I want to make love to you because you're the most beautiful person in the world."

"You think that? You really think I'm the most beautiful girl in the world?"

I could sense that my words had mollified her.

"You're the most lovely gorgeous adorable creature that has ever existed in the whole of history. Since time began. Venus has nothing on you."

"Am I more beautiful than Vivien Leigh?"

"Vivien Leigh is not fit to be your slave," I said.

Julia relaxed and smiled at me. "You can be quite nice when you want to."

"I'm sorry I couldn't contain myself any longer," I said, hurrying to follow up my advantage by eating humble pie.

"You're forgiven."

"Am I in with a chance?" I asked, daring to produce another outburst of disapproval.

Again she smiled at me. "Perhaps. I'll have to think about it," she said. "And now what about something to eat? I'm absolutely starving."

Lunch was a success. Although Julia preened herself as usual, and made herself the center of attraction to the best of her ability, she occasionally deigned to listen to me. I knew something was on her mind.

When we came to the end of the meal I said: "Do you mind if I have a brandy?"

"Of course not," she said.

This was odd. Usually she disapproved of my drinking spirits. She never drank anything but wine, and I believe that later on in her life she gave this up and turned to fresh fruit juices.

I was sipping my brandy when she said: "Michael, I've got a wonderful idea."

"Let's hear it," I said.

"Let's go to Paris for Christmas."

I was sure that this meant that she had considered during the course of lunch the future of our relationship, and had come to the conclusion that I was in danger of pulling out, unless she did something about it.

Without hesitation I said: "That's a wonderful idea."

My immediate reaction pleased her. She leant across the table and touched my hand. "You're really rather sweet."

"Have you been thinking about it, about us?" I asked.

"The answer is still perhaps," she said, reminding me of a tart trying to extract the maximum amount of cash from an inebriated customer.

"Where shall we stay?"

"What about the Ritz?"

"But we'll never get in."

"Leave it to me," she said. "I've got a friend at the Embassy and he'll be able to pull the strings."

For a moment I wondered if this friend at the Embassy was one of her lovers and she was about to use me to get a free ride to Paris. But I told myself that jealousy would in no way help me to achieve my object.

"When shall we go?" I asked.

"Just as soon as I can fix it. And, Michael, let's go on the Golden Arrow. That would be fun, wouldn't it?"

"It would be romantic too," I said determined to keep Julia aware of the fact that I adored her, and wanted more than anything else in the world to sleep with her. As I gazed at her with a dog-like devotion, I could visualize the most intimate parts of her body as she slowly removed her dress and underwear.

"Do you think, Michael, we could do one other thing? I would like to ask you now before we go. I don't want you calling me a gold digger when we get there."

I had now mentally completely stripped her. "Anything you want, my darling," I croaked.

"Could I buy a few clothes, just a few?"

"I will buy you the Ritz if you want it."

"You are very, very sweet, Michael," she said.

The word "perhaps" had turned to "yes."

"There's only one problem about buying clothes," I said. "There's a twenty-five pound travel allowance."

"Don't worry, Michael," she said. "I'm sure my friend at the Embassy will know how to get round those silly old regulations. You're really sure you would like to buy me some clothes?"

"Of course. Why do you ask?"

Julia hesitated. "Well they won't be cheap. I mean, I would simply love something by Dior. You know about him? He's the latest thing. I really would love to wear the New Look."

"Darling, you can have what you want," I said determined to press home my advantage. I think I rather spoilt the effect by adding: "Within reason, of course."

Julia must have reckoned that she had got me pointed in the right direction and that I would give no trouble. "Then, my dear, that's all agreed. Oh, it will be such fun to buy some decent clothes for a change."

Before we left the Savoy we had arranged that she would telephone Paris, arrange a suite for us at the Ritz, and book two seats on the Golden Arrow.

My joy knew no bounds when, before I put her in a taxi in the forecourt of the Savoy, she put her face up to me to be kissed. Not wishing to chance my luck I discreetly avoided her lips and pecked her velvety cheek.

I walked down the Strand in the twilight, not noticing the freezing air or the snow which had begun to fall. I was certain that all would be well; that my time and money had not been wasted. Julia was about to be mine. How wise I had been not to count the cost.

I stopped a taxi and asked the driver to take me to Dolphin Square. All the way I thought of Julia. Would she be good in bed? She would be wonderful. Perhaps I was about to embark on the great love affair of my life. Steady on, I told myself. You know perfectly well that you do not love Julia. You lust after her. In a minute you will be offering marriage, and marriage with Julia would contain the seeds of its own dissolution. You would be bored stiff if you had to live with her permanently. Make her your mistress. In that way you will stay mad about her. And don't fool yourself. She doesn't love you one little bit. She is using you. But two can play at that game. She has something to sell at a price and you are prepared to pay for it.

All the way in the taxi I could see her face on the other side of the table and hear her RADA trained voice murmuring sexily: "Perhaps. I'll have to think about it."

I could not help thinking about it.

When I got out of the taxi in Dolphin Square, I was distraught with anticipation and the most lurid fantasies.

I did not know what I was doing.

A voice in the dusk called gently to me: "Want a good time, darling?"

I was mad. "Yes, I certainly do," I answered.

She came out of the shadow and put her arm through mine. A few minutes later she was in my bed and I was sprawled across her.

To this day I cannot remember what she looked like. All I can recall was that her name was Jasimine. That's what she told me. But she did not smell at all sweet.

Oh Jasimine, what a disaster you were to turn out to be.

Julia and I left by the Golden Arrow for Paris on December 21, 1946 with the idea of spending Christmas there and returning to England in time for New Year's Eve in London. She had taken the precaution of booking a table at the Savoy where we had decided to welcome in 1947.

Cyril Connolly wrote that one of the great joys in life is to drive South with someone you love. I prefer those old fashioned trains with their dark panelled carriages, uniformed attendants, delicious food and drink which gave me the feeling that I was not in this world. They have now all disappeared. Today the object of travel is to get you to your destination with the maximum speed. Air travel has taken over from the railways, and as fewer and fewer travellers have opted for the luxury of the wagon-lits, so they have gradually been forced out of business.

As the Golden Arrow pulled out of London, it was snowing hard. I felt an immense inner warmth, and every time I glanced at the beautiful girl sitting opposite me, I could not believe my luck. Nor could I contain my excitement as I imagined what joys lay ahead in the privacy of a suite at the Ritz in Paris.

By the time we had reached Dover and transferred to a private cabin on the boat, we had drunk two bottles of the best champagne and eaten a full breakfast. The English people might be severely rationed, but this did not apply to the plutocrats who could afford first-class fares on the Golden Arrow. The service was attentive. I have noticed that waiters are always much more solicitous when I am travelling with an attractive girl. I must also confess that I feel flattered. It is comforting to know that one's taste is approved of, and besides, it is good for one's ego especially when one is middle-aged. On the other hand, when one is past fifty it is probably wiser not to be seen about with nubile nineteen and twenty year olds. This can produce mutterings of "Dirty old man" in the ranks of the waiting staff.

The only minor disaster on the Channel crossing on a British boat was that the purser was unable to produce champagne. The sight of a five pound note had not the slightest effect. But the sea was calm. We took one stroll on deck, but the Arctic conditions were too much for us, and we returned to the warmth of our cabin, where for the remainder of the voyage I sat on the edge of Julia's bunk while we chatted amicably. When we had docked at Calais and had boarded the Paris express, I could see no obstacle to prevent me attaining my objective. I had concentrated all my available forces with a skill worthy of my old general, Montgomery, and had avoided the error of dissipation.

There was a slight hitch at the Gare du Nord. I was forced to carry our luggage. Luckily Julia was travelling light, no doubt intending to re-stock her wardrobe during the course of the next few days. But how to lay my hands on a taxi presented a serious problem.

There was no sign of a queue. Hundreds of screaming Frenchmen and Frenchwomen milled around in a disorderly mass, cursing barging and hitting one another with sticks, umbrellas, and heavy pieces of luggage. As a taxi came into the station, long before it had discharged its passengers, the waiting mob would converge upon it, wrench open the doors and try to fight their way inside.

I was disgusted by this exhibition. I have always thought of France as one of the most civilized nations in the world. But as women and children were knocked to the ground, which was covered with slush and grit, I began to wonder what had happened to them. Had they been completely brutalized by the German occupation? I could not help thinking of Lord Grantley who, although he held some minor post in the British Government, always insisted on travelling in a French boat. When asked by reporters what was the reason for this, he replied: "Because in French boats there is no nonsense about women and children first." The spectacle before me confirmed his words, but I believe he was relieved of his post for making the remark.

It was very cold as I stood surveying the scene and I felt Julia shiver. The situation called for action. Nothing would be achieved by waiting. I had no intention of allowing myself or Julia to be trampled to death by the rioting crowd.

I picked up Julia's luggage in one hand, and put my arm round her waist.

"We'll get nowhere standing here."

"What?" she shouted above the noise of the howling mob.

I pulled her along the pavement and made our way out of the station in the direction from which the taxis were approaching. Luck was on my side. In the main street outside the station there was a large hotel. Hurrying forward against the snow, I pushed open the revolving doors and we went inside.

From that point all was plain going. A number of francs were pocketed by the hall porter with instructions to telephone the Ritz and ask them to send a car to pick us up. I reckoned that the Ritz would not fail to do this for a customer who was staying in one of their suites that had been booked by a big wig at the Embassy. I was right. Half an hour later, after a further donation of francs, our cab was splashing its way through the streets of Paris en route for the Ritz.

"That was brilliant of you," said Julia as she leant against me for warmth.

"I remembered what my old soldiers would have advised. Never get involved in any sort of fighting. There's always a way round. The generals found that out at Cassino. After they had lost thousands of men trying to attack it from the front," I said.

"What on earth are you talking about?" she said.

I did not answer. Our taxi drew up in front of the Ritz and we got out. A few minutes later we had been shown into our suite. It consisted of a bedroom, a sitting room and a large bathroom. There was a double bed in the bedroom, and I was relieved when Julia made no adverse comment about it. I told myself that she must have reserved a room with a double bed when she had given her instructions to her friend at the Embassy, which could only be good news.

"Look, darling," she said, "I'm going to have a bath right away. Why don't you order something nice?"

I was almost sure the double bed was no mistake when she said this. It was the first time she had called me darling in all the time I had courted her. When she went into the bathroom, closed the door, but did not lock it, I was absolutely certain. My great hour was approaching.

I ordered champagne as suggested, and was sipping it in the sitting room filled with lascivious thoughts when I heard Julia moving about in the bedroom. For a moment I considered that this might be the moment to launch the attack, but on second thoughts decided against it. I had not yet bathed myself. I went to the bedroom door and knocked on it.

"Come in," Julia called.

She was lying on the bed wearing a thin dressing gown, through which I could see the contours of her perfect figure and the delicate texture of her skin.

For a moment I thought I would be unable to control myself. All my animal instincts cried out to be let off the rein, having been held on a strong leash for so long.

Julia knew what was racing through my mind. "Why don't you have a bath, darling?" she said sweetly.

This was the second time she had called me darling. My joy was infinite.

"Darling, I adore you," I said. "Will this really be our night?"

She nodded, smiling so sexily that again I had to restrain myself from leaping on her there and then.

"But don't let's hurry. It will be better for waiting, won't it?"

I did not disagree although this seemed a fatuous remark almost akin to her having no respect for herself if she gave herself to me like a common tart.

She further spoilt the effect by adding. "Anyway, I'm absolutely starving. While you bath I'll get dressed. Then we'll go downstairs, have a drink in the bar, and then eat in the restaurant."

I did as I was bidden. I went into the bathroom, stepped out of my clothes, and lay in the hot water trying to calm down by thinking of everything except Julia and the night of love with her that lay, after all my trials and tribulations, only a matter of a few hours ahead. But nothing could remove her from my mind. My fantasies became cruder and cruder. My excitement mounted second by second.

When I went back into the bedroom, not even the Turkish towel draped round my waist could conceal the state I was in. Julia could not have failed to notice, and I wondered if she would have the kindness of heart to put me out of my agony. But it was not to be. She was hungry and the consummation of our love would have to wait.

The events of the next two hours are hazy. I do not wish to keep harping on the subject, but the truth is that all I could think of was making love to Julia.

Julia enjoyed herself immensely. Even though the bar was full of well-dressed women, she was the center of attraction. I felt male hostility in the air. Clearly most of the men in the bar were asking themselves how did a paunchy young man manage to get off with such a wonderful looking girl.

"Tell me about this bar," said Julia. "It's terribly famous isn't it?"

"It was in the twenties and thirties. Scott Fitzgerald used to get boozed up here. It was a favourite haunt of Hemingway. Of the two he's by far the most important. Personally I think he is one of the outstanding writers of the century. His only fault was to have had a disastrous effect on his imitators."

Julia was not interested in my thoughts on Hemingway. She stood up and said: "You can take me into dine, darling. I hope you've booked a decent table where I can be seen."

She took me by the arm, and as we drifted through the bar in the direction of the restaurant I knew that I would never in my whole life have a finer hour.

I cannot recall what we ate. This is proof enough that I was in an advanced state of insanity. Usually I remember places and persons by meals. For instance I first visited Venice in 1937. I have no recollection of the great churches or paintings, although I wore my feet to the bone tramping round and gazing at them. Venice 1937 is epitomized for me by heaps of fresh scampi at Jimmy's bar, washed down with a cool Frascati from the Alban hills. I can still taste each one of them.

It is with difficulty too that I can recall what happened in the bedroom, where eventually I found myself in a dazed condition soon after ten o'clock. I know that was the time because Julia had placed her travellers' clock on the table by the bed. I remember thinking to myself how considerate of her it had been not to linger too long over the coffee. She must have known the agony I was suffering and was hastening to give me blessed relief.

I took her in my arms and kissed her gently. I knew that I must not be too rough or advanced. I made no attempt to slip my tongue into her mouth. In any case I was happy enough to be holding her, even if I was shaking like a leaf.

"Am I beautiful?" she asked.

I nodded. I was speechless.

"Say I am beautiful," she said.

"You are the most beautifulest girl in the whole world," I managed to stutter.

She disengaged herself from my arms.

"You get undressed in here, and I'll go into the bathroom and take off my face," she said. "I must never forget my face wherever I am. So many actresses ruin their careers by forgetting to look after their complexions."

When she reached the bedroom door, she turned and said. "Tell me again that I am beautiful."

"You are more beautiful than Aphrodite."

Julia frowned. "I don't like the sound of that. Who is this Aphro ... or whatever you said?"

"Aphrodite ... the Greek name for Venus," I said.

She smiled. "That's all right then," she said.

I pulled back the top sheet and blankets, stripped off my clothes, leaving them in a crumpled heap on the floor. I lay on my back on the bed listening to the thumping of my heart and wondering if by some ill chance I was about to suffer a coronary.

I heard her come into the room. I was so paralysed with excitement that I could not turn on to my side but lay on my back like a fish our of water, gasping for breath.

"My God, you're hard," she said.

"I'm dying," I said. "I'm dying, Egypt."

"I like it," she said.

To this day I do not know if she was referring to my reference to Shakespeare which came into my head for no good reason, or simply to my cock.

To my amazement she climbed on to the bed and straddled her legs either side of my body. Looking down at me she said: "You deserve a real treat tonight." She leant forward so that her long hair fell across my chest, then slowly she started to move her mouth towards my loins, licking me with her tongue.

I can remember thinking it incredible that this dream of beauty should be actually going down on me. After all this was 1946, and oral sex had not yet appeared on our cinema screens.

I felt her tongue move just below my belly. Fears of premature ejaculation flooded in on me, and I desperately thought of the cold nights of the Italian campaign, and the first day I had been called up into the Army at Inkermann Barracks, Woking.

Suddenly all hell was let loose.

With a scream that might have wakened the dead and must certainly have wakened everyone staying in the Ritz Hotel in Paris on that night, she leapt off me and raced to the bathroom door.

Here she paused and turned on me, crouching and spitting like a cornered cat.

"You filthy bastard," she shouted. "You filthy bastard. You've got the fucking crabs."

"Darling..."

"Don't darling me," she hissed. "Just get dressed and piss off."

"Where can I go...?"

"You can go to hell for all I fucking care. Just leave my tickets on the dressing table and my share of the travel allowance and get out. I never want to see you again. You might have ruined my career. Do you realize that? You could have ruined my career, you stinking bastard."

"Can't I stay...?"

"No you cannot," she yelled. "And what is more if you haven't cleared out by the time I've had a bath and managed to make myself clean I'll shout the place down and tell the manager that you tried to rape me."

She disappeared into the bathroom, slamming the door behind her.

I have always known when I am defeated. A brief examination of my lower area proved that Julia had spoken the truth. Why I had not noticed or felt them before is still a mystery. Possibly my mind had been entirely concentrated on Julia and the delights that lay ahead with her, to the exclusion of all else.

There was nothing to be done. There was no point in attempting to hold an untenable position. I had not the slightest doubt that if I did not clear out, she would come back and start shouting rape. It could have been very nasty indeed.

I did as I was bidden. I left her tickets and twenty-five pounds in cash on the dressing table. There was no time to pack properly. I decided to come back the next day when she had gone, and collect the rest of my clothes. I put on my suit and overcoat, made my way downstairs and out into the Place Vendôme. It was bitterly cold and snowing hard.

I cannot remember what I did that night. I must have wandered round Paris and visited a few bars. But I was too miserable to get drunk. It was not until about six in the morning when I was sitting alone and nearly frozen solid in a small bar in Les Halles that I asked myself where on earth I had picked up those little monsters.

Then I remembered a voice from the shadows calling to me: "Want a good time, darling?"

Oh Jasimine, why couldn't you have kept those blighters to yourself?

Oh Jasimine, how rightly you punished me for my sins.

At nine o'clock I decided to return to the Ritz. I was shivering with fever and so tired that I could hardly keep my eyes open. Yet at the back of my mind had returned a hope, however faint, that Julia might not have left and might even forgive me.

I went into the hotel and asked the Hall Porter if she was upstairs.

"Madam left at seven this morning."

"Oh," I said.

He must have noticed my stricken state for he added: "Madam took a taxi to the Gare du Nord."

So that was that. Julia had gone back to England.

I collected the key of the suite and took the lift upstairs. I went into the bedroom and noticed that the sheets and blankets on the large double bed were exactly as I had left them. In the sitting room next door the champagne which I had ordered to keep us refreshed through the delights of the night, was still in its bucket uncorked. The sofa was piled high with cushions and it was obvious that Julia had spent the night there as far away as possible from the claws of the monsters. I touched the pillows which so recently had given comfort to that beautiful body, and as I did so the tears started to roll down my cheeks.

Unable to control myself I threw myself upon them sobbing loudly and shaking all over.

In the course of the morning I gradually recovered. I kept asking myself what my drivers would have done in my situation. Clearly the position was irretrievable. The answer was to cut one's losses. There was no point in wasting money at the Ritz. I knew only a few people in Paris. At least back in England I would have friends or acquaintances to keep me company over Christmas.

Having come to the decision to leave France, the next problem was one of disinfestation. I got out my ancient phrase book to see if it could be of any help. But whereas it obligingly told me how to say in French that the postilion had been struck by lightning, nowhere did the useful phrase "I have been stricken by crabs" appear.

Did one go into the chemist's and say: "*Monsieur, je suis attaqué par les crabes.*"

Somehow it did not seem right to me. I had a vision of myself lying on the beach and hordes of large crabs sidling towards me, with outstretched claws.

I tried to think of an alternative word for crab. Suddenly the answer came to me. Louse, plural, lice. For the first time in my life I thanked the French master at my preparatory school, who had made me learn the French for hundreds and hundreds of words that I would hardly ever be likely to require in the course of my life. Words like lawn mower, peacocks, vacuum cleaner, navel, safety valve, and louse. I could see it before me: *Pou* s.m., *poux* pl.

I tried again. "*Monsieur, je regrette beaucoup que je suis attaqué par des poux formidables.*"

On consideration from all angles I liked it. I especially admired the fact that I *regretted* and that the lice were *formidables*. Ten minutes later, armed with my phrase, I was out of the Ritz and into the nearest chemist.

Waiting for the opportune moment when I would be served by a man rather than by a girl, I darted to the counter: "*Monsieur,*" I whispered, "*je regrette beaucoup que je suis attaqué par des poux formidables.*"

For a moment I thought that all was lost; that he had failed to understand my accent, or worse, that my choice of words had been incorrect.

Suddenly he smiled. "*Ah, monsieur, très très formidables,*" he said, pointing to his chest and lower regions.

I found myself copying his action and nodding vigorously, until I noticed a well-dressed woman standing a few feet away staring at me in amazement.

Swiftly he took a small bottle from the case behind the counter, wrapped it in white paper and passed it to me.

"*Combien, monsieur?*" I asked.

"*Rien,*" he replied still smiling. "*Avec les compliments de la maison.*"

"*Bon Noël, monsieur,*" was all I could think of saying in answer.

I have been accused by people of having pursued a love affair with France all my life. I plead guilty. With a memory of a kindness like that who can blame me? I declare and will stand by it that the French are the most civilized people in the world.

Ten minutes later I was in the bath in my suite at the Ritz shaving myself all over. As I watched the hairs disappear down the plug hole I could not help asking myself whether such disasters ever struck Hemingway or Scott Fitzgerald in the course of their association with the Ritz Hotel in Paris.

# 8

I spent the Christmas of 1946 at the Salisbury. George Holmes on my return had sensed that something had gone drastically wrong, and invited me to stay there as long as I wanted. And like the gentleman he was, he made no reference to Julia. He must have realized that, as she had not put in an appearance at the pub, our affair, if one can call it that, had busted up.

Early in the New Year, Raymond Mould who had been publicizing a tour in the provinces where I presume he had spent an alcoholic Christmas and New Year, came tottering into the Salisbury one morning.

"Right, we're off to see Tony," he announced to me after he had downed a double gin.

"Tony?"

"Tony Vivian. My Lord Vivian. My old partner. You'll like him. I suppose you don't remember you agreed to come and work for me a couple of weeks ago."

"I didn't think you meant it," I said.

I had imagined it was one of those offers that are often made by people when they are in their cups, and meant to be forgotten the following morning.

Tony met us at Brockenhurst station and drove us to his house. I cannot remember much about the two days I spent there. Tony was on his own, and at one point we went out to the local pub, returned laden with bottles, and proceeded to tear a roasted chicken to bits. I was particularly fascinated by a pair of Queen Victoria's shoes or slippers that she had worn as a little girl, which were displayed under a glass cover. I did learn a little about Tony. He had served in the Merchant Navy, and had conducted a dance band at the Ritz during the twenties or early thirties. At one time he had been an habitué of Rosa Lewis's hotel, the Cavendish in Jermyn Street, on whom it is said the successful television series the Duchess of Duke Street was based. Rosa Lewis on one occasion got Tony into serious trouble with his father. He was staying there one night when Rosa took it into her head that he had offended her. She picked up the telephone and called his father at his stately home in Cornwall.

"Listen, my lord," she screamed down the telephone, "I've got that no good bloody son of yours staying here, and he's upstairs in bed with a tart."

Tony's sister, Daphne, married the Marquis of Bath. After they were divorced she married Ian Fielding, and wrote a book about Rosa Lewis. Sometime during that autumn Tony took me to meet Rosa Lewis whom of course I had read about in Evelyn Waugh's novels. I was disappointed. She was sitting in a pokey room off the hall, a small and frail old lady. Tony bought her a bottle of champagne, but I do not think she recognized him. The hotel was dark and dingy. It was difficult to imagine it had once been the haunt of the Bright Young Things. The old Cavendish eventually was pulled down and a new hotel built on its site. One of its bars is called the Rosa Lewis bar, and I wonder how many of its customers today know the reason why.

On our way back to London I was gratified when Raymond told me that Tony had approved of me. I can only assume that this seal of approval was based on my ability to consume vast quantities of alcohol.

It was on the day that we returned to London from visiting Lord Vivian in the country that Raymond took me for the first time to his office. Previously I had not even known that his firm possessed such a thing. It was situated on the second floor of a block of Edwardian buildings in Great Windmill Street, famous for its theatre, the Windmill, "which never closed." It had remained open all through the Blitz on London when every other theatre in town put up its shutters.

The office consisted of one room, sparsely furnished. There were a couple of chairs, a desk with a telephone on it, and last year's calendar hung in shreds on one wall.

"Like it?" said Raymond.

"It's all right," I said, not wishing to express my true feelings and cause offence.

"It stinks," he said.

He went to the desk, picked up a pile of messages, and thumbed through them muttering to himself. Looking over his shoulder I read: "Mr Cochran telephoned." "Mr Sherek telephoned." "Mr Olivier telephoned." There must have been at least a dozen in similar vein. Some had been marked Urgent, while others had been marked in red Very Very Urgent.

Having glanced through them Raymond dropped them into the waste paper basket muttering, "Silly cow," as he did so.

"Who's a silly cow?" I asked.

"Joan, my secretary. You haven't met her and you don't want to. She's sheer misery. What's more she's pregnant."

"By you?"

"Don't be disgusting," said Raymond. "By some second rate bloody actor."

"Don't you do anything about those messages?" I asked.

"Not bloody likely. If only people would stop pestering me."

"But they're your clients aren't they? I mean don't you ever do anything about them?"

"Look, Michael, if you take any notice of them, they start clamouring for more. Believe me, once you've got them on your back, you'll never get them off." He opened the drawer of the desk, and took out three envelopes and proceeded to extract the cheques inside them. They were for amounts of five and ten pounds.

"Well, that's enough work for the day," said Raymond. "Let's go and cash these round the corner."

The sight of men queueing outside The Windmill theatre as we made our way to a pub was sufficient to bring on Raymond's spleen.

"Just look at the silly buggers," he said making no attempt to lower his voice, "Queueing like bloody sheep just to see a bit of tit half hidden by a fan, so that they can wank themselves off under their disgusting macintoshes."

Fearing that we would be violently assaulted at any moment by those sex starved gentlemen, I took Raymond by the arm and hurried him past them and guided him into the nearest bar, where he continued to acquaint the customers with his opinion of the Windmill and its clients.

Having cooled down he went to the bar and cashed the three cheques. It seemed to me an odd way to run a business.

"Don't you keep any books?" I asked.

"I leave that to my accountants."

"They must have quite a job preparing a statement if all your incoming cheques are presented at hostelries all over London."

"Please don't be a bore," said Raymond. "If you are going to work with me, you must promise not to discuss money."

"Can I ask if I will get paid, and how much? Then I will never mention the subject again."

"Would ten pounds a week and expenses be all right?"

"It seems fine to me."

Raymond handed me two five pound notes. "That's the first week. Let me know if you need any more."

During the time I worked, if that is the word, with Raymond, I always had to ask him for money. It was not that he was mean about it. He just hated it and regarded it undignified of the human race to handle the stuff. For him it was a necessary article of barter to be exchanged for gin as quickly as possible. When I finished working for Raymond I was several hundreds of pounds out of pocket in the way of expenses. The difficulty was that there was no way of claiming them. I tried to work out a system with Joan, his secretary, but the trouble was that as soon as any cheques came in, Raymond would grab them and hurry to the nearest pub to cash them. When I mentioned the subject to Raymond he would stare at me dolefully, and hand me a five pound note with a look of extreme distaste. I have no doubt that a psychologist would say that Raymond suffered from an advanced anal fixation.

As we drank in the pub that morning Raymond told me something of his business. As I have explained previously, his job was to get free publicity for the shows his clients put on either in London or on tour in the provinces. It seemed to me at the time that Raymond had most of the theatre publicity business in his hands. Certainly all the big names were on his books, although the word "book" may be an unfortunate choice, as he kept no records whatsoever. His filing cabinet was his waste paper basket.

Raymond was paid a flat rate per show, which was either five or ten pounds per week. He was not very keen on the former, and gradually eliminated what he called "those mean bastards." I suppose at the time I joined him he had about two hundred pounds a week coming into his office. This must be the equivalent of well over a thousand pounds a week today, and it is still a mystery to me as to why Raymond was always broke. I suppose he gave it away to anyone who looked down and out or in need of a meal or a drink.

There were plenty in the theatre in those days and there still are.

As far as I could make out, none of this income ever went through a bank. I believe at one time Raymond had dealings with the National Provincial Bank, but after the departure of Lord Vivian, Raymond had decided to dispense with its services altogether.

Raymond's methods of publicizing his clients' shows were three. There were the first night parties. It was his job to ask the drama critics and to provide them with free drink in a bar especially set aside for them. I was to discover that Raymond did not just invite the critics. He asked along any journalists he liked, or indeed any convivial characters in or outside of Fleet Street he happened to bump into during the course of the day. He was also responsible for posting hand-outs to the provincial Press extolling the virtues of a production and naming its stars. In fact he hated doing this so much, considering ninety per cent of his shows utter shit, that he left it to Joan. His third function was to be a bridge between his clients, their actors, and Fleet Street. I was to discover that this was about all he did, although it brought him little relief from his melancholy. He would wander into newspaper offices, pubs, and dressing rooms, bearing bad news.

To the theatre correspondent on the *Daily Express* he would declaim mournfully: "There's a frightful show called *Pain in My Arse* coming into London next week. The cast are abominable, and the whole thing is utterly dreary. On no account go near it."

People in general loved Raymond, and I never knew a journalist let him down. *Pain in My Arse* would receive a fantastic amount of pre-publicity, which would make Raymond even more miserable and more active in venting his hatred against it to all and sundry. Generally speaking he reserved his adverse comments for journalists, and was far less outspoken with the actors and actresses. To begin with he really did love the theatre and those who worked in it. He was aware of their insecurity, and to him they were always children to be treated as such. I think the only time that he was really happy was when he was lolling about in a dressing room gossiping, although he tended to be boring about the past.

There were in early 1947 other theatre publicists operating, but Raymond had by far the largest share of the business. One of the big companies he did not promote was that of H. M. Tennant, which under impresario Binkie Beaumont together with John Perry, dominated the theatrical scene. Their publicity was in the hands of Richard Clowes, who had an office in the same building as Raymond. They were on very good terms with one another, and Richard Clowes was quite content to look after H. M. Tennant, and showed no desire to expand his business.

Richard Clowes was living at the time either in John Gielgud's or John Perry's house in Lord North Street. He complained bitterly of the cold and had christened them Frigidaire Mansions. It was a source of irritation to him that he was charged rent for his room, and at every opportunity he would berate one or the other for their miserliness and for daring to charge an old friend for his accommodation.

Through Richard I frequently met Binkie Beaumont, John Perry, John Gielgud, Alec Guinness and many other Tennant stars. Binkie and John Perry would lunch most days at Victor's Restaurant in Lower Wardour Street. It was only a short walk from their offices at the top of the Globe Theatre in Shaftesbury Avenue. These could only be reached by a very small lift that creaked its way up ominously, and was the source of much ribaldry. Victor's was a small French restaurant where I had eaten regularly before the war. It had not changed at all. The food was very good and I can still hear Victor himself calling the orders down the hatch to the kitchen. For some reason I can still hear in particular his voice chanting *"Deux potages."*

From the day I started to work for Raymond, I realized it could not last long. To begin with I knew very little about the theatre, and if anything I tended to despise it. But the real trouble was that Raymond had no method of work. He was a drifter. I do not think that even he knew from one minute what he would be doing the next. He treated his clients like dirt. On the other hand he obtained a great deal of publicity for them. But the more he procured for them the more he swore at them and neglected them. He particularly disliked the few stars he had taken on to promote personally. I never did discover why he had even promised to get them publicity in the first place. It may simply have been that he needed the money. Woe betide any of them who had the audacity to telephone him to ask him to take some kind of action. Invariably he struck them off his list. The result was that I found myself trying to work in an atmosphere of utter chaos. Matters were not helped by Joan, who was a naturally untidy and indecisive girl. She would have been a good secretary to an organized boss. With Raymond she went to pieces. She looked perpetually distraught and unhappy, and very often sat at her desk weeping for hours on end. She was terrified of the telephone, because every time it rang she knew that on the other end would be some impresario or actor trying to get in touch with

Raymond. She, of course, never had any idea where he was.

"Yes, Mr Cochran. Certainly, Mr Cochran. Mr Mould will be coming into the office some time later today and I'll be sure to give him your message. Yes, yes, Mr Cochran, just leave it to me. I'll personally make sure he telephones you."

As soon as she had put down the telephone she would look at me with swollen eyes and say: "But Michael, what can I do? Everyone thinks it is my fault but I do my best to look after Mr Mould. The trouble is that he just refuses to do anything. He won't even write a cheque out for the electricity bill and it'll be cut off and he'll blame me and tell me it's all my fault. What shall I do, Michael? What shall I do?"

Poor Joan. She was one of the world's losers, and she had every reason to be depressed. She should have walked out on Raymond. The trouble was that she loved him. She was on a losing wicket. The more she tried to help him and cosset him the more he shrank away from her. In the case of the electricity bill, for instance, she became so anxious that she finally paid it out of her own wages. When she informed Raymond of what she had done he flew into a rage.

"How dare you insult me," he hissed at her. "How dare you! I can perfectly well manage to pay my own bills without interference from you."

This was manifestly untrue. Raymond never paid a bill until the last possible moment. Solicitors' letters were stuffed into his pocket and later transferred to the waste paper basket. Court orders were ignored until the bailiffs turned up at the office. Joan would lie through her teeth on Raymond's behalf, saying that he was in New York or Hollywood, and she was sure it had been an oversight on his part, and she would be sure to see that he sent a cheque as soon as he returned. It was something of a mystery to me how Raymond managed to keep out of the debtors prison and I must admit that I gradually began to get irritated at the way he frittered his money away and threw business down the drain.

A classic example of his disregard for business was an incident concerning Vivien Leigh. She had decided, because she liked Raymond, that she would ask him to take on her personal publicity. Accordingly after several days of trying to get in touch with him without success she arranged through Joan that Raymond would meet her in the bar of the theatre where she was appearing, after the curtain rang down. Raymond was extremely angry with Joan for daring to commit him to this appointment but grudgingly agreed to keep it.

On the day on which Raymond was to meet Vivien Leigh I had a premonition that all would not be well. As he proceeded to swim through the day in a trough of gin he became more and more morose.

"I can't be bothered with the silly bitch, Michael," he kept mumbling to me. "She gets all the publicity she needs and will be nothing but trouble ringing me at all hours of the day and night. You know, Michael, all I want is peace and quiet."

This seemed to me an extraordinary statement coming from a theatre publicist, but I held my peace, and did my best to steer him through the day, determined to get him to the theatre to meet Vivien Leigh as had been arranged.

Just before eleven we both tottered into the theatre much the worse for drink. I assumed that our client-to-be must have known of Raymond's habits, and was anxious to be publicized by him, gin and all. We staggered into the empty bar as the audience was leaving. There was no sign of Vivien Leigh.

"Just like a bloody actress to keep us waiting," said Raymond. The bar was closed and locked as the show was over. This was a personal insult to Raymond.

"She not only has the nerve to keep us waiting. She's too mean to buy us a bloody drink."

I tried to reason with Raymond. I pointed out that she was almost certainly changing after the show.

"Then why didn't she ask us to meet her in her dressing room?" he demanded.

This was a reasonable question and one I was never able to answer.

At this moment Vivien Leigh came smiling into the bar.

"Ah, there you are at last, duckie," said Raymond.

"How sweet of you to come, Raymond," she said. "How are you, my dear?"

"I'm all right, duckie," he said swaying from side to side. Then pointing a finger at her he continued: "But you were bloody awful, duckie. Bloody awful."

"What on earth ..." began Vivien Leigh.

"Shut up and let me speak, duckie. I saw your performance tonight and it was a disgrace. I remember the day, duckie, when you were out in front of the house selling programs, and that's bloody well where you should be today."

I have seldom seen anyone look so surprised as Vivien Leigh. But she controlled herself admirably and said: "Good-night, Raymond. It was kind of you to take the trouble to come." With which she turned and walked out of the bar.

"Silly bloody cow," muttered Raymond. "Let's go and get a drink."

Needless to say, Raymond did not secure Vivien Leigh's business. Why he chose to insult her, he refused to inform me. He had not been near the theatre that evening, and had never seen her in that particular show. As far as I know she never in her whole life sold a single program.

Life was never dull while I was with Raymond. It is impossible to describe a typical day, because no day was ever the same. In trying to do so I can only link together memorable events which took place in the two months I spent in his company.

I went to the office about eleven and was greeted by a tearful Joan who was already snowed under with messages and bills from the day before and the day before that. She made me a cup of tea and poured out her troubles. And her troubles outside the office as well as in it were endless.

Soon after eleven Raymond telephoned asking for me.

"But Mr Mould, you simply must come into the office. There's stacks ..."

I heard Raymond shouting down the telephone. "I want to speak to Michael, not you."

She handed me the telephone and started to cry.

Raymond told me which pub he was in. I grabbed the cheques that had come in that morning and went to meet him.

He took the cheques and exchanged them across the bar for pound notes.

"Let's get out of this stinking dive," he said. "I suppose we might as well go down Fleet Street as anywhere else."

Ten minutes later we were inside El Vino. Raymond surveyed the crowd of journalists and did not like what he saw. "What a terrible place this is," he announced to the bar in general. "Just look at all these silly sods who think they are important and shaping the fate of the world. All they come here for is to fiddle their expenses."

For the next half hour Raymond spread gloom and despondency concerning the state of the theatre and his own productions in particular. It occurred to me that there was possibly a streak of genius in his technique. Journalists tend to shy away from publicists who are always boosting their goods to the sky. I do not think I ever heard Raymond say a good word about any of his productions. The result was that the journalists told themselves that they could not possibly be as bad as he made out.

Suddenly Raymond decided that he had had enough of El Vino for one morning and weaved his way through the throng out into the street where he stopped and muttered, "There must be some better way of earning a living."

I was beginning to come to that conclusion myself. "Frankly, I don't know how you manage to keep going," I said.

"Nor do I. Where shall we go?" Without waiting for an answer he pulled the collar of his old R.A.F. overcoat round his shoulders, and dived across the road into another pub.

The bar was deserted. This pleased Raymond, who smiled for the first time since I had met him that morning. "I have come to the conclusion," he announced, "that the only trouble with the world is that it is inhabited by the human race. Let us swear that we will avoid all contact with people as far as possible from now on. It really is so much nicer in this deserted bar without all those silly sods shouting their head off about subjects they know nothing about."

"That's all very well," I said, "but I must remind you that we have a first night at seven this evening."

"Let's not go."

"But Raymond, we are there to ensure that the critics and other hangers on have a good time and write us good reviews."

"The play is a load of shit," announced Raymond.

"You're in the wrong job," I said irritably.

"Have you only just found that out?" he said. "Oh, Michael, I'm so utterly bored."

By reminding him of the first night that lay ahead I had plunged him back in to the depths of despair. I think it was then that I knew my days working with Raymond were strictly limited. His moods of depression were becoming infectious.

"Come on, let's go down to the Salisbury and see if Richard Clowes is there."

We found Richard at the bar of the Salisbury, blue in the face with cold, wearing his blue overcoat which had already started to collect its daily quota of ash down its front.

"Before I forget," said Raymond, "would you like to be bored by the most appalling play tonight?"

"If the theatre is heated I will sit through anything," said Richard.

"There will be plenty of whiskey too," I added.

"In that case I accept your kind offer," said Richard. "What is this extravaganza that you are attempting to promote, Raymond?"

"I'm not sure."

"It's a play by Turgenev," I said.

"Raymond has never heard of Turgenev. He probably thinks it's some kind of Russian gin," said Richard. "And what other delights have you in store for the unsuspecting public, Raymond?"

"Oh, do shut up," said Raymond. "Can we have a drink in peace without talking about work?"

"You've never done a day's work in your life, Raymond," said Richard. "Unless, of course, you call running away from life, work. The trouble with you, Raymond, is that you have no powers of concentration, except weeping into your glass of gin. Will you have another one, by the way?"

"Oh, I suppose so, if you insist."

The morning was becoming like all the mornings that preceded it, and like all those that were to follow. I felt myself drifting senselessly on a cloud of alcohol, with no purpose or direction. What was worse I was unable to make any effort to fight back. It was only about one o'clock in the afternoon and I could already predict what lay ahead. I could forsee the disasters, the endless rounds of drinks, the rows, and Raymond's increasing gloom that would inevitably envelope me.

As usual we did not eat anything at all. We visited a few more pubs and at each one Raymond's dislike of his fellow creatures increased. Finally, for some inexplicable reason, Raymond announced that he had decided to reform his ways and intended to return to our office in Windmill Street.

"I bet you won't stand it for more than half an hour," said Richard.

"Oh, shut up," said Raymond.

As we passed the crowds queueing outside the Windmill Theatre, Raymond could not resist discoursing in a loud voice about little men who carried macintoshes with them.

Richard went to his own office down the corridor and Raymond led the way into his. For a moment I thought that Richard was right, that Raymond would not stand it for three minutes, let alone thirty. He visibly winced as Joan said: "Ah, there you are at last, Mr Mould. Just look at these messages, hundreds and hundreds of them."

The telephone started to ring. She picked it up.

"I'm not in," Raymond hissed at her.

"Yes, Mr Sherek. Mr Mould should be back any minute. Yes, Mr Sherek, I'll be sure he calls you. Yes, he does have a first night. Good-bye, Mr Sherek."

"Oh, Mr Mould, you don't know ..."

"Just be quiet, and take this dictation. What's the name of the horror we have opening at Nottingham next week?"

"*Cloudless Summer*, Mr Mould."

Raymond put his face between his hands rocking from side to side. "Next week playgoers in Nottingham will have the pleasure of seeing the brilliant new comedy *Cloudless Summer* ..." He paused and I could see that his heart was not in his handout. "Where was I, Joan?"

She read what he had dictated back to him. "With an all-star cast headed by Susie Smith and Peter Nelson, *Cloudless Summer* will be making a short tour before coming to London. The story is set in Venice and centers round the romance of an allied spy for an Italian dentist."

"Dentist, Mr Mould?"

"Peter Nelson has got beautiful teeth," said Raymond. "Oh shit it all. You take over Michael."

"But I haven't even read the script, let alone seen the play. You refused to allow me to come to the rehearsals."

"I didn't want you to puke," said Raymond.

"Oh, please, please try to be serious," said Joan. "These releases must go out tonight."

"You write them, duckie," said Raymond.

I heard the door open and turned in my chair to see Richard smiling benignly.

"What a pretty scene. Did I hear the sound of work? I must have been mistaken."

"I'm trying to write a release for *Cloudless Summer*. Please, please go away," said Raymond.

"Oh, come, come. You mustn't work so hard. How far have you got? I bet it starts something like this: Next week theatre-goers in Shitsville will have the pleasure of seeing that brilliant new comedy *Cloudless Summer*. With an all-star cast ... and that's a downright lie ... *Cloudless Summer* will be making a very short tour before coming into London's West End."

"Oh, go away," moaned Raymond.

"You know you'll never finish it. It's all a load of crap anyway. Come on, you know what you really need is a large gin to steady your nerves. *Cloudless Summer* can look after itself."

"Oh, Mr Clowes, please don't take Mr Mould out of the office."

"I'm only doing him a kindness, dear," said Richard. "He detests this office. You'll come too, won't you, Michael?"

I looked at Raymond and knew there was no hope for us. Five minutes later we had crossed the street and climbed the stairs to Mac's Club. No sooner had we arrived than Raymond swore loudly. "I promised to be at the Adelphi at three."

"What on earth for?" asked Richard.

"C. B.'s auditioning for *Bless the Bride*. Come on, Michael, we must hurry."

This was one of the few occasions that I ever saw Raymond the slightest bit distressed because he had let a client down or ignored an important appointment. I think it was because he had a very soft spot for Cochran who was also extremely fond of him.

We left Richard at Mac's Club, and were lucky enough to find a cab to drive us through the snow to the Adelphi.

We went into the auditorium where Cochran was sitting in the stalls about six rows back. I had already met him on several occasions and what had struck me about him was the great courtesy he showed to everyone. His old-world manners were very much in evidence at this audition. He knew as soon as one of the girls auditioning had opened her mouth whether she was good enough to be short-listed. And although he did not allow those who were clearly not good enough to sing for long, he cut them short as politely as possible by saying: "That was very nice, my dear. Thank you so much for taking the trouble to come along."

After the auditions and a few words with C. B., Raymond and I made our way to the theatre where the Turgenev was opening. The temperature was below freezing, and on arrival we found the theatre only half heated due to a shortage of fuel. People were already arriving wearing everything they could lay their hands on and looking more like scarecrows than first-nighters. Raymond, who was still wearing his R.A.F. overcoat, looked slightly less incongruous than usual.

The first-night bar had already been laid out in a private room by the house manager.

Raymond inspected the meagre sandwiches, and counted the numbers of bottles of beer and spirits.

"Mean bastards," he commented. "If they think they'll get good reviews on this lot, they must be raving mad."

I still do not know how much the supply of free booze affected the critics' judgment or their notices. I do not like to imply that they were all a bunch of mercenaries who could be swayed by a tot of Scotch. Nevertheless, in a time when drink was in short supply, there is no doubt that it put some of them into a good mood. Generally speaking the posh papers were incorruptible. The critics of the popular Press had very little space in their papers for reviews, so what they wrote mattered little one way or the other. I suspect they came along for the free seat and the odd drink or two. On the whole I think those first-night bars were a waste of money. About a year later the theatre managers and impresarios reached the same conclusion and discontinued them.

Among the critics there that night were Harold Hobson and James Agate. I have always thought the former one of the best critics to have worked for *The Sunday Times*, although somewhat infected by French flu. But as I have already written so am I, except that I am addicted to French food rather than to the French theatre. I never enjoyed Agate's criticism or his autobiographical books which he published under the title of *Ego One*, *Ego Two*, and so on. I consider them overrated and boring. Certainly they have not weathered the years. He was too in my opinion the worst possible type of critic, who always tried to shine at the expense of the object of his criticism. I have always thought many critics are writers who have not made the grade, and being witty or bitchy about people more productive than themselves is their only compensation.

I remember on that particular night that Agate drank a bottle of whiskey, and spent little time in the theatre. The next day there appeared a glowing review under his signature. This only depressed Raymond further.

These first-night gatherings of the theatre critics were tame compared with the lavish parties laid on for the film critics. These were held in grand restaurants like the Hungaria, and nothing was deemed too good for them. I went with Raymond to several of them, and was amazed at the richness of the food and wines supplied. Post-war Britain might be blanketed in austerity, but there was no sign of it at these banquets. There was still an atmosphere of the Hollywood of the thirties. It was as if a war had never taken place. One of the disasters of the film industry has been its inability to admit that any kind of change ever takes place. Even today it tries to ignore the fact that television is today's entertainer. The film industry still tries to fool itself that while attendances are dropping annually by millions, in some miraculous way known only to itself, its prosperity is increasing.

Apart from the shortage of food and drink in post-war England, there was a general lack of all kinds of domestic articles, from saucepans to frying pans, knives and forks. In the case of saucepans, the fault was Lord Beaverbrook's. As Minister of Aircraft Production he had organized a collection of aluminium kitchen utensils, telling the public that they could be melted down to make vital aircraft. This was scientifically impractical, and the country was littered with mountains of kitchen equipment that would have been better employed had it stayed in the kitchen. On the other hand it is arguable that Beaverbrook's appeal engendered a wave of patriotism. Dumps of pots and pans, along with the railings removed from round the parks symbolized the determination of the British people to win the war and not to count the cost.

As a result of these shortages these film parties were much loved by certain critics, journalists and others who managed to wangle invitations, or penetrate the security net which surrounded them. A number of the guests saw absolutely nothing wrong in stuffing their pockets with knives, forks, silver platters and entrée dishes, to obviate the shortages caused by the recent war. Others contented themselves with smuggling out vast quantities of food, whole chickens, tongues and hams. In the end the situation became so scandalous that some of the film companies were forced to engage security guards to frisk the departing guests. I shall never forget the sight of an eminent film critic being forced to disgorge from beneath his overcoat a whole roast turkey. Further tapping of his pockets brought forth half a dozen knives and spoons bearing upon them the insignia of that particular restaurant.

The day following the first night of the Turgenev play, I spent the morning and the afternoon at the office trying to sort out some of the messages, many of which were a fortnight old. There was no sign of Raymond, but he telephoned me about midday instructing me to meet him at the Vaudeville Theatre at seven, where one of the shows he was publicizing was running. When I tried to get him to turn his attention to one of the hundred pressing matters, he hung up on me. I appreciated that Joan had a difficult life. I advised her there and then to dry her eyes and look for another job.

"But what will Mr Mould do without me?" she sobbed.

He did not seem to be doing very much with her, but I refrained from saying so.

I telephoned several of the more infuriated clients, and tried to pacify them with little success. Most of them did not know that I was working with Raymond, and those that did declined my offers to help and begged me to make sure that Raymond got in touch with them immediately. The effect of this was to make me feel unwanted. I had to face the fact that there must shortly be a parting of the ways, that I could not drift along for ever with Raymond, trying to pick up the bits, that—to put it bluntly—the world of theatre publicity was not for me.

Soon before seven I set out to walk to the Vaudeville. The streets were slippery and where the snow had fallen and had not been properly swept up, it had turned into solid ridges of ice. People hurried by looking miserable. The street lights were only on in a few places, and the illuminations had been turned off by an order of the government to save coal at the generating stations. Once again I muttered to myself, Oh my God, what a way to win a bloody war.

At the Vaudeville Theatre I found Raymond in Gordon Harker's dressing room. They were both bemoaning the fact that things were not what they used to be. I had to agree with them. As soon as Gordon Harker had to go on stage we made our way to the bar upstairs, where we had a chat with the House Manager. It seemed that business was not too bad in spite of the Arctic conditions that were paralysing the whole country. The main problem was that of heating the theatre. I could not help wishing that I still had a platoon of my drivers on hand. If there was coal to be had it would have been delivered without fail to the theatre the next morning if not that night.

After a few drinks we left the Vaudeville and fought our way through the snow to the Adelphi next door where Cochran was presenting *Big Ben*. As soon as we went into the foyer and heard the sound of music from beyond the doors that led to the stalls, Raymond cheered up. For some reason he had developed a sentimental attachment to that particular show. It had been written by A. P. Herbert, with music by Vivian Ellis. It had a kind of gusto and gaiety that appealed to people in those dreary days.

The real reason that Raymond enjoyed visiting the Adelphi may have been that Harty, his favourite theatre barmaid, ran the stalls bar. We made our way through the auditorium and went into Harty's bar. A. P. Herbert was already there with a glass in his hand. I had met him through Raymond and was to meet him several times over the next few years, and develop a great respect for him. As an independent member of Parliament he had succeeded in starting the reform of our archaic divorce laws which were strongly slanted against women. He was to be a strong supporter of Lending Rights for authors.

No sooner had we come into the bar than the orchestra in the theatre swung into the main theme song of the show. Without more ado A. P., Raymond and I began to belt out:

> I want to see the people happy,
> I want to hear the people sing.
> I want the sun to shine on England.
> Oh, the things that I would do if I were king.

We were so carried away by our performance, that having joined in with the chorus in the theatre, we forgot to stop when the leading lady started her solo. From the theatre came shouts for silence, but we sang on:

> I want to see the people happy,
> I want to hear the people sing.

The door of the theatre bar was pushed open, and through it I could see the audience in the stalls looking in our direction.

"Please, please, sir, could we have a little hush. In any case for God's sake keep it down a bit," implored one of the theatre commissionaires.

Before the curtain rang down, after a final *sotto voce* rendering of the chorus, A. P. bid us a cheerful good night and left.

Raymond and Harty chatted about the old days and theatre bars they had known, and before we departed Harty extracted a promise from us that we would go and have Sunday dinner with her at her flat south of the river.

This was one of the few engagements that Raymond managed to keep without being dragged along by me. He might have let the

King of England down, but not Harty. "She's lovely, absolutely lovely," he kept telling me. We met in the West End and set out in a taxi soon after midday. Unfortunately soon after we had crossed Waterloo Bridge, Raymond caught sight of a pub with its doors open, and he insisted that we go in to fortify ourselves against the cold. Luckily for him there was a fair supply of gin on tap, although I had to content myself with a couple of glasses of watery beer. By the time we left at one o'clock, he was beginning to show signs of an early deterioration.

Eventually we found Harty's flat and Raymond paid off the taxi with wads of notes. Once he had secured the services of a taxi he would never let it go, however long he had to keep it waiting.

Harty had laid on a magnificent spread. She must have known her way round the local Black Market. There was a sirloin of roast beef, Yorkshire pudding, roast potatoes and vegetables, followed by apple pie and cream. I watched Raymond's look of fear grow as she heaped his plate high. When she had put it in front of him, he could only pick at it with his fork. He did not put one morsel into his mouth.

"You poor thing you," said Harty getting up and going to the cupboard. She took out a bottle of gin and put it on the table beside him and removed his plate.

"There you are ducks," she said. "That's what you really like for your dinner, isn't it?"

"Thank you, Harty. You are the sweetest person in the whole world," said Raymond. A tear ran down his cheek.

It was around the end of February or the beginning of March 1947 that Mr Stein began to torment Joan at the office. Not content to leave a message once a day for Mr Mould to telephone him, he began calling at hourly intervals.

"Whoever this bloody man Stein is, tell him that on no account do I wish to know him," shouted Raymond one morning when he had deigned to put in an appearance at the office.

"Aren't you even interested to know what he wants?" I asked.

"No I am not."

"Couldn't Michael call him and try to find out what it's all about?" suggested Joan.

"No, he cannot. I just will not have people pestering me," shouted Raymond. Noticing that Joan was about to cry he turned to me and said: "Let's get out of here. This place depresses me."

A couple of days later I came into the office at about eleven to find a stranger wrapped in an expensive fur coat sitting on the only spare chair. I noticed the electric fire was not burning.

"I'm afraid there's been another power cut, Michael," said Joan. "This by the way is Mr Stein."

Mr Stein stood up and held out his hand. "How do you do?"

"Alive if nearly frozen to death," I said.

"Your office is not exactly palatial is it?" said Mr Stein.

This remark annoyed me. "Mr Stein, we do not waste our clients' money on fixtures and fittings. We aim for results."

Mr Stein beamed. "Ah, that is very good news. I hope then you will be interested in my proposition. But first, where is your Mr Mould?"

"Mr Mould is in Hollywood talking with Warner Bros.," I said. "He will be returning via New York. In his absence I am fully qualified to act on his behalf. What can I do for you?"

"I have had the most excellent reports of Mr Mould through my theatrical friends. They tell me he is the best publicist in the business."

"Absolutely. No one to touch him," I said.

"I will come straight to the point," continued Mr Stein. "You may have heard of my firm, the cosmetics firm of Stein & Stein."

"Naturally. The whole world knows of Stein & Stein," I said.

"Come, come," said Mr Stein. "That cannot be true. We are only a very small operation at the moment."

Thinking that I had overstepped the mark and shown too much enthusiasm for the firm of Stein & Stein, I hastily added: "By the whole world, I mean that part of the world that matters. Anyway, what can we do for you, Mr Stein?"

"First of all let me ask you a question," said Mr Stein. "Is it true that Mr Mould knows everyone in the theatre? Is he a friend of all the stars?"

"Indeed he is. An intimate friend," I said. "There isn't a single star in the entire constellation who does not adore Raymond. You name them, they love him. Vivien Leigh worships him, Laurence Olivier comes to him for personal advice. The Lunts wine and dine him when they are in London, and Edith Evans asks him to hear her lines. Bob Hope and Bing Crosby rely on him for their personal publicity."

Mr Stein held up his hand. "That is enough. It is what I had been told. Now my proposition is this. In two weeks' time we are opening our new shop in Bond Street."

"To sell your cosmetics?" I asked.

"Exactly. And I want that opening to go with a bang."

"Of course you do," I said. I was not stupid and could see how Mr Stein's mind was working. "And you want a galaxy of stars at your *première*."

"You have hit the nail on the head," said Mr Stein.

"How much?" I asked.

Mr Stein looked taken aback at the directness of my question.

"Don't let's beat about the bush," I said. "Time spent in haggling is always wasted."

"First of all we would make it worth while the stars attending, and would be willing to supply them with a year's free make-up."

"Very fair," I said.

"Naturally we should expect them to visit our premises in Bond Street, so that people would see them going into them."

"I like it," I said. "You should have been in the publicity business yourself. I don't see that you need us."

"But Mr Mould knows the stars."

"Every single one of them," I said. "Now, what about our fee?"

Mr Stein eyed me. "Two hundred pounds."

"It seems reasonable," I said. "I shall of course have to finalize it with our financial director."

The telephone started to ring. Joan picked it up. "It's Raymond for you, Michael," she said. I grabbed the receiver and jammed it against my ear. "Hello, Raymond. How's that bastard Warner behaving? I bet you screwed the last penny out of the old sod."

"What the fucking hell is going on . . .?"

"Great, great," I shouted. "And Bing? Give the old sod a kick in the pants from me."

"What the hell . . .?"

"Listen Raymond, I can't talk now. I'm tied up with a client. Give my regards to all at the New York office . . ."

"Get the cheques out of the drawer and come on over to the back bar at the Café Royal," screamed Raymond.

"That's great, great," I shouted. "It sounds a wizard contract to me. Perhaps we could get a new office . . . You what? No, I guess you're right. No use wasting money on carpets and furniture . . . That's right . . . We go for results."

"Oh, get stuffed," said Raymond and slammed down the receiver.

"Sorry about that, Mr Stein," I said. "Oh, yes, about our fee. Two hundred pounds and of course all expenses will be chargeable to you."

"Expenses?" said Mr Stein and I thought he looked slightly anxious.

"Little matters like champagne at the opening and a few bits and pieces to nibble. We will of course arrange all that with our caterers. Then I suggest an intimate party at the Savoy for the stars."

Mr Stein was beginning to panic but I was determined to play for high stakes. If this was the last thing I did for Raymond Mould, I was determined to go out in a blaze of glory.

"Look, Mr Stein, you just cannot be mean with the stars. If you want bit-part actors to come to your opening, I can get you hundreds for peanuts. But it won't do you any good. You will be throwing money down the drain. If you want the best we will supply them, but the best is never cheap. Like your fur coat for instance. A splendid coat if I may say so, and you didn't buy that for shillings."

I could sense that the thought of all those stars was too much for Mr Stein. I was right. He held out his hand. "I'll do it," he said.

I shook his hand. "Leave it to me," I said. "As soon as I have spoken to my financial director I'll come back to you. There will of course be the matter of an advance payment on our usual terms. Fifty per cent in advance and fifty per cent on completion. That includes both our fee and estimated expenses.

"Fifty per cent seems ..."

I ignored Mr Stein and swept on. "May I suggest Vivien Leigh, Laurence Olivier, Robert Morley who as you know is now playing the lead in *The First Gentleman*, Edith Evans possibly, and I believe Katherine Hepburn, a great friend of Mr Mould's, is staying at the Connaught."

"Excellent, excellent," said Mr Stein. "Thank you so much for your assistance. Give my warmest regards to Mr Mould and tell him how much I look forward to making his acquaintance."

When Mr Stein had gone Joan looked at me and wailed: "What have you done? Oh, what have you done?"

"A fine piece of business."

"But all those names, Michael. All those names."

"Raymond knows most of them, doesn't he?"

"Yes, he does. But he'll never get round to asking them. What's more Mr Mould will hate the idea, absolutely loathe it."

Joan was right. Raymond was positively hostile towards me when I informed him of the remunerative business I had transacted with Mr Stein.

"You wait and see, Michael. He'll be nothing but trouble," he moaned. "I know that type. Tight-fisted Jewish bastards. You wait and see. Shylock has nothing on your bloody Stein."

"But think of that two hundred pounds."

"I must admit that's not at all bad. And I liked your piece on the telephone. Have you ever thought of being an actor, Michael?"

"Never."

"A pity. Can I leave it to you to make all the necessary arrangements with Mr Stein? After all he's your friend. Be sure to get the advance money out of him before you do anything on his behalf."

"You'll lay on some stars to satisfy him?" I asked.

"There you go already causing me worry and extra work. I have a nasty feeling that Mr Stein is going to be nothing but a load of trouble."

"You do want to do this promotion? You do want that two hundred pounds?" I said.

"Don't be so ridiculous. How could I not want two hundred pounds?"

In the course of the next three days I worked like a slave on Mr Stein's and Raymond's behalf. I laid on the caterers, selected a suitable buffet for the eleven o'clock morning opening of Mr Stein's new premises. I called on the banqueting manager at the Savoy and arranged for several tables to be reserved in the grill room at lunch time to accommodate a galaxy of stars. I wrote glowing hand-outs extolling the virtue of Mr Stein's products. I can honestly say that I did everything in my power to make the operation an outstanding success.

The only drawback was Raymond. Whenever I tried to talk to him about Mr Stein or suggest that it was time he set about roping in a handful of stars to attend the opening ceremony and to proceed afterwards to the Savoy where they would be seen lunching with Mr Stein, he flew into a temper. "Leave me alone, Michael. Can't you leave me alone? I hate your Mr Stein and never want to see him or even hear about him for that matter."

"But Raymond, Mr Stein has behaved like a gentleman. Only this morning he had a cheque delivered by hand, a hundred pounds in advance for our fee, and another hundred towards the cost of the food."

"What about the Savoy? Who's going to pay for that?" grumbled Raymond.

"I have no doubt that Mr Stein will behave like a gentleman and settle the bill when the occasion arises," I said.

"Mr Stein is no gentleman. How can a man who causes so much trouble even consider himself to be one?"

I knew that I was beaten; that Raymond for reasons known only to himself had turned against Mr Stein.

As the day of the opening ceremony approached my anxiety turned to panic. All that I had succeeded in doing was asking a few unknown actors, and a couple of out-of-work journalists to attend the great opening. All of them had agreed to put in an appearance attracted by the prospect of unlimited free drink and a luncheon at the Savoy.

My life was not made any easier by repeated and desperate telephone calls from Mr Stein asking for the guest list. When he threatened to come round personally I advised Joan to bolt the door and sit in the dark so that he should not see a light under the door.

I must admit that Joan behaved admirably. She stopped crying. For the first time since she came to work for Raymond, she found the situation funny. She entered with me into the spirit of that amazing operation. She even learned the art of lying to Mr Stein, inventing all manner of imaginary clients who were constantly keeping me and Raymond out of the office. She apologized profusely to Mr Stein, promising him that all would be all right on the day.

On the night preceding the gala opening I had reached a pitch of hysteria. I did not know whether to laugh or cry. I considered the best thing to do would be to leave London. I envisaged myself having to flee across the Channel before criminal proceedings were started against me. No jury could possibly bring in a verdict of Not Guilty. I had lied. If ever there was a clear cut case of false pretences, this was it.

We were having a drink in the upstairs bar at the Vaudeville Theatre when I made my last appeal to Raymond.

"If you don't do something about asking a few names to the party tomorrow I am leaving town this minute."

Raymond looked at me mournfully. "I told you that Mr bloody Stein would be nothing but trouble."

"I am asking you for the last time to do something or I quit."

"Oh, all right then. But what a nuisance it all is. We might as well start here."

We made our way to Gordon Harker's dressing room.

"Gordon," said Raymond. "I've come to ask you to do me a favour. There's a dreadful fellow called Stein promoting his revoltingly useless make-up at his tatty little shop in Bond Street tomorrow at eleven. There will be lashings of free champagne and a slap-up lunch at the Savoy afterwards. If you've nothing better to do, please come along and be thoroughly bored."

We visited about ten theatres that evening, and that was the gist of Raymond's invitation to stars, bit players and chorus girls alike. I cannot say that I was optimistic about the result as far as the stars were concerned but it seemed to me highly likely that we would have every chorus girl in London in Bond Street the next morning.

Towards eleven at night Raymond lost interest.

"What about a few journalists?" I implored him. "We must have a few from Fleet Street to write up this momentous event."

"Oh for God's sake, Michael, belt up. We'll make a short sharp sweep down Fleet Street tomorrow at opening time and rope a few in."

I was tired and apprehensive. When Raymond suggested we go and get something to eat I declined his invitation, and took a taxi back to my flat in Dolphin Square where I spent a sleepless night.

At half past ten I went into El Vino where we had agreed to meet, and was surprised to find Raymond already there. He seemed cheerful enough, and my spirits rose for the first time for several days.

"Have you asked any journalists?"

"Don't be bloody silly. I've only had one gin. Don't worry. I told you last night there was no problem."

As the early morning drinkers came in, Raymond wandered up to them and repeated his invitation of the night before, adding in each case: "Bring along anyone you like. It should be a fair old piss up."

We left El Vino and called at a couple more pubs in Fleet Street where Raymond distributed invitations to anyone who happened to be near.

"Well, I think that about does it. One more call at the Salisbury and your bloody Stein should have a full house."

I looked at my watch. It was already twelve and the opening had been due to begin at eleven.

At the Salisbury Raymond gave up any attempt to ask actors, actresses or journalists, but contented himself with marching up and down the pub shouting: "Free piss up for anyone who fancies it. Stein and Stein, cosmetic shop in Bond Street. You're all welcome."

As we left the Salisbury and got into a taxi he turned to me smiling and said: "Guess that should just about leave standing room only. Stop worrying, Michael."

I find it difficult to recall that day, partly because of its nightmarish quality, and partly because in the end there was only one answer and that was the bottle.

I remember arriving at the shop in Bond Street to find it already packed to the doors. We forced our way through the mob towards the bar. I noticed that the buffet had already been stripped bare as if it had been attacked by a shoal of piranha. To mark the occasion Mr Stein and his fellow directors were all dressed in morning clothes and were standing in a corner viewing the scene with panic in their eyes.

"Silly buggers," shouted Raymond. "Think it's bloody Ascot or something dressed like bloody Christmas trees."

Soon after we arrived the looting began. I do not think that's too strong a word. It started with some out-of-work actor picking up one of the special packs that had been made up as presentation gifts for the stars. This was the signal for everyone to do the same, and in a second the hundred boxes of expensive make-up had been seized by the avaricious chorus girls and boys.

Mr Stein fought his way towards me.

"Mr Nelson, what is going on?" he shouted. "Where is your Mr Mould? I must speak to him."

"This is Mr Mould," I said indicating Raymond who was downing a tumblerful of gin.

Mr Stein looked at the swaying figure next to me draped in an old R.A.F. Officers overcoat.

"Mr Mould," shouted Mr Stein, "I have not yet made my speech. I must make my speech. I must make my speech."

Above the noise of the howling mob Mr Stein could not hear Raymond's reply. I did. "Then fucking well make it," muttered Raymond.

I had to do something. I leapt on to the table which only a short time before had been laden down with rich food and was now completely bare, and yelled at the top of my voice. "Let's fucking have you!"

There must have been some old soldiers in the crowd, for these well-known military words of command produced a momentary hush. I followed up my success by shouting. "A little bit of quiet please for a few words from your host, Mr Stein."

Regretfully the silence for Mr Stein was not sustained for long. The guests ignored him and turned their attention to consuming or hiding beneath their coats what was left of the drink.

"Ladies and gentlemen of the theatre," I dimly heard Mr Stein say, "On behalf of my directors I welcome you to this opening of Stein and Stein cosmetic ..."

Someone in the crowd yelled: "Bollocks."

Someone else shouted: "To the Savoy."

On all sides the cry went up: "To the Savoy. To the Savoy."

"I suppose we might as well go along," said Raymond. "I'm so glad they seem to be enjoying themselves."

I do not remember seeing Mr Stein at the Savoy during the course of that riotous luncheon. But I do recollect that some fifty people sat down and ordered the best food and wines that the hotel could supply.

Raymond drew up a chair by my side. "I think it's so clever of you to lay on such a distinguished gathering," he said.

I tried to focus my eyes, and through a haze of alcohol, looked round the restaurant. One thing was certain. There was not a single star present.

About three o'clock Mr Stein and his directors still wearing their morning coats put in an appearance. The waiters had just started to hand round the boxes of cigars and to bring on the brandies.

With a cry of horror Mr Stein started to rush round the tables snatching the cigars out of the hands of the guests. It was an ugly scene. I decided to follow the advice of my old drivers and retreat in the face of a potentially dangerous situation.

I turned to Raymond. "Good-bye, Raymond," I said. "I resign." I rose unsteadily from my chair.

Raymond looked up at me and smiled. "What a pity," he said. "You might have made a good publicist in time. But you would have hated it, like me."

# 9

For two days after my attempt to promote Mr Stein's organization I lay shivering in bed in my flat in Dolphin Square. The heating had been turned off; there was no hot water in the taps. Through the window facing my bed I stared at the grey sky and the falling snow. The wind howled and I threw everything I possessed on top of the bed and tried to sleep but with little success.

I ate nothing. There was no drink in the flat and I did not even have the energy to go in search of a bottle of whiskey on the Black Market. It was hunger that eventually forced me to get up. I looked in the cupboard in the kitchen and discovered a couple of mouldy soya link sausages which I heated over the gas stove. But my stomach was unable to accommodate them. Having thrown them up I returned to bed.

I suppose by this time the effects of the last months' intake of alcohol were beginning to wear off and I fell into a fitful sleep. I do not know how long I slept but it could have been as many as three days.

Strangely enough, when I emerged from that deep sleep I found that my depression had faded. I was even able to look back over the events of the last six months with a kind of detachment. Admittedly they had not been the happiest or the most successful months of my life, but I told myself as I had reminded myself so often during the years I had soldiered overseas that at least I had survived.

There was still no hot water in the flat, but I scraped off my beard as best I could in cold water and went out in search of something to eat.

I was lucky to chance on a café with a friendly waitress. It must have been about eight in the morning because it was still dark, and I was the first customer.

She took one look at me and said: "Blimey, you don't half look bloody awful."

"I've been ill."

"I should bloody well say you have, ducks. Looks to me as if you've been half bloody dead. Here, let me get you a cup of tea."

I was so overcome by this display of kindness that I nearly broke down and wept.

She brought me a cup of steaming tea. "I've put a whole week's sugar ration in it for you, ducks. They say there's nothing like hot sweet tea to bring back the dead. What's your name?"

"Michael."

"Well fancy that now."

"What's so odd about my name?"

"My boy friend was a Michael. I called him Mick. Lovely boy, he was."

"Was?"

"Yes, was, ducks. Copped it at Dunkirk. A long time ago now and the funny thing I always think that one day he'll come back. To tell you the truth I thought it was him that came in just now when you walked through the door. You look a little bit like him, though of course you're much older."

"I'm twenty-five."

"You could have fooled me," she said. "Look more like forty-five to me."

"I've been away a long time," I said.

"Was you a soldier?"

"Some people wouldn't say so. But I was in the army if you see what I mean."

"Here, let me get you something to eat and then you can tell me all about it. Look as if you need someone's shoulder to cry on. What would you say to a couple of real boiled eggs, none of that nasty dried egg powder rubbish?"

She came back in ten minutes later with the eggs and four slices of bread and butter. She put them in front of me and sat down at the table opposite me. "Get stuck in, soldier," she said. "By the way my name's Mavis, but everyone calls me Mave."

My encounter with Mave was one of the most providential in my life. There were no other customers in the café during the next half hour. It was not until, in the course of our conversation, Mave mentioned it was Sunday that I realized that the majority of Londoners were battened down for the day and had no intention of braving the hostile elements. During that half hour I was able to recount to Mave much of what had happened to me since I had returned to England. It was not until I had finished that I realized how much I had been in need of someone to whom I could pour out my heart.

"Now you've got that lot off your chest, Mick, perhaps you could tell me what you propose to do next?"

"Think."

"Thinking won't bring in the cash, Mick. By the way, where are you living?"

"Dolphin Square."

"That's bloody posh. How much do they rock you there?"

"Eighty quid a month."

I thought Mave was going to faint on the spot.

"Eighty bloody quid a month. Eighty bloody quid. Listen, Mick, you can forget that straight away. You're leaving that dump now. Eighty quid for a poor bloody soldier home from the war."

"I've nowhere else to go."

"Oh yes you have, Mick. You're moving into my place tonight, and that's for bloody certain."

"But I can't. I mean ..."

"Shut your mouth. If it's your bloody pride you're thinking of, forget it. I shall be glad of a couple of quid a week off you."

"But a couple of quid ..."

For the first time Mavis was angry. "Belt up. A couple of quid, that's all I need and all I am asking. Right, listen to me. Go back to your flat and pack your gear. Have you got much?"

"About a suitcase full."

"Good. See you back here at five this evening when I knock off."

I leant across the table and tried to kiss her.

She pushed me to one side. "Get away with you. You don't have to do that."

That evening I moved into Mavis's room in a bombed house in Lupus Street, where I was to stay for the next few weeks. It was small and sparsely furnished, but scrupulously clean. Mavis would dust it every morning before she left for work, and at week-ends she devoted a couple of hours going over it from top to bottom. She took great pride in her few possessions.

In the mornings I made myself breakfast and every evening she cooked a hot meal. She was never short of food, and I presumed, although I never asked, that she brought it back from the café where she slaved. Slaved is the right word. For a working week of fifty-five hours she was paid the princely sum of five pounds.

As there was only one bed in the room we had to share it. There was no hardship in this because we helped to keep one another warm. With my overcoat piled on top of the blankets we were able to build up a fair amount of heat. On one particularly cold night we even drew the floor rug over ourselves but found it too heavy.

About the third night I stayed with Mavis I made the mistake of making a pass at her. We were lying in one another's arms and I started to feel her breasts. She stiffened. I stupidly assumed this was in anticipation of further delights to come. I started to move my hand down across her flat belly in the direction of her crotch.

"Don't," she said fiercely. "Don't."

"I thought you'd like me to make love to you," I said.

"I want no such thing. You don't fucking love me so don't fucking pretend."

Mavis seldom swore, and I knew by her language that she was cross with me.

To make matters worse she started to cry. "I'm sorry, Mick," she said as I felt her tears on my cheek. "Oh, I'm so sorry. But I'm so lonely since my man never came home and everyone thinks I'm easy game and tries to go to bed with me. But I still don't fancy anyone but him. Does that make sense to you?"

"Yes. It makes sense. But you can't go on loving a dead man for ever."

"That's what they all say. But I can. I can. It's no good everyone telling me I can't, if I do. Do you see what I mean, Mick?"

Looking back I suppose I was the nearest thing she ever found to her dead soldier. She had told me that I looked like her Mick, and that's why she called me by his name.

It was the day following this incident that I paid a visit to my bank to draw some cash. While I was there I asked for a statement of my account and found that I was still four hundred pounds in credit. As I walked up St Martin's Lane to the Salisbury one thing became clear to me. Once again I must face up to the necessity of getting some kind of a job. I could not live for ever with Mavis, apart from the fact that I was getting bored living alone with my own company all day. Since my several days of drying out in the flat in Dolphin Square after the Stein disaster, I had been drinking very little. I had no intention of frittering away the remainder of my capital for the sake of companionship in the bars of London.

Inside the Salisbury I was warmly greeted by George who demanded to know where I had been for the last couple of weeks. He had heard about the Stein affair, and told me that Raymond had left London with a company that would be on tour for several weeks to avoid Mr Stein's fury and a flow of solicitor's letters that had started to pour into his office by every post.

In spite of the snow and icy streets the Salisbury was full.

When I commented on this George said: "Of course, too bloody cold for the tarts to operate outside. Every pub in the West End is jammed with them. This place is nothing but a pick-up center. Nothing I can do about it but keep the boys apart from the girls, so that they don't start arguing over clients and getting the nail files out. Oh, by the way Raymond told me to tell you that if you're passing his office to call in and collect a few pounds he feels he still owes you."

I had a couple of beers with George then left and made my way towards Piccadilly Circus. George had spoken the truth. The Circus was almost deserted by the prostitutes, and when I turned into Windmill Street I was surprised to see a queue of men waiting outside the theatre. God, I thought, men will do anything for the sight of female flesh. What did they get for their money, I asked myself. On an impulse I joined the queue. My luck was in. No sooner had I done so than there was an exodus from the theatre. I must have arrived at the interval between the shows. After only a ten minute wait during which I was nearly frozen stiff, I found myself inside the relative warmth of the theatre.

When the show came on I was disappointed. It consisted of a number of indifferent vaudeville acts. As for the nude shows they could have been put on at any Sunday school without giving offence. They made the exhibitions I had seen in the Middle East seem the height of pornography. I just could not believe my eyes that grown men would pay to see a girl weaving a lot of fans in front of her body, not exposing so much as a tit. Even the climax was tame in the extreme. As a grand finale she would lower her fans to reveal for a brief second her nude bosoms, and then with a final flick of her wrist stand exposed as the lights went out. Even then she was still wearing a G string.

I left the theatre mystified. I was about to enter the building where Raymond had his office when I stopped dead in my steps and swore aloud.

I have been told that great ideas come to people at the oddest moments, such as when shaving, bathing, hanging up the washing, or touching one's toes. Mine came to me at no particularly strange moment. It came as a logical sequence after watching that puritanical exhibition at the Windmill theatre.

I would parade girls completely naked, pubic hairs, pudenda, the lot. If men would pay for the glimpse of a G string, what wouldn't they pay to see everything? The idea was so simple that I wondered why no one had thought of it before.

For the next twenty-four hours I considered my idea from all angles. I made a few enquiries, and discovered that to do what I proposed would be outside the law. So what, I asked myself? Prostitution and soliciting were illegal, but the police made no effort to stamp it out, except for pulling a few girls into court each morning where they were fined five shillings by a bored magistrate.

My next job was to find myself a partner. My obvious choice was John Fish but as he had been stupid enough to sign on in the army for a further period, he would have to suffer the sight of my becoming a millionaire while he rubbed along on his army pay. There was certainly no one I had met in my wanderings around London who filled the bill. The trouble was that I could think of no one I could trust.

I was about to give up and had decided to go ahead on my own when I suddenly thought of Driver Tibbs, my old batman who had succeeded Driver Lane, and whom I had encountered when I had driven down with George to the East End to pick up a consignment of wine. Even his words came back to me: "If you reckon you're tough enough, a little brothel business would be the best thing to invest in."

The advantage of my idea was that I would not even have to lower myself to the position of becoming a brothel keeper. In any case I remembered that Tibbs had commented that the brothel market had already been taken over by the Sicilians and Malts and that anyone trying to muscle in might end up with a knife in his guts. Like Tibbs I hated the sight of cold steel. My idea was something new, something that the Malts and Sicilians had not yet got on to.

Luckily I had kept the telephone number of Tibb's employer. I spoke briefly to Tibbs, intimating that I had a matter of the utmost secrecy and profitability to impart to him, and arranged that he should meet me that evening at the Café Royal.

Tibbs I am glad to say took to the idea like a duck to water. As we relaxed in our chairs sipping the best brandy that the Café Royal could provide he looked at me with admiration in his eyes: "You're a fucking genius, Captain. A fucking genius, that's what you are. It's so bloody obvious. I can't see why some other bugger has not thought of it before."

"It's like the wheel. Do you know there was a time, Tibbs, when wheels didn't exist?"

Tibbs was not interested in this philosophical speculation on my part. "Look Captain, you say you can put up two hundred quid. I can't match that but I'll put up a hundred and come in for twenty-five per cent of the profits."

"Wouldn't dream of it," I said. "Fifty-fifty, or nothing."

"You silly sod," said Tibbs. "Now let me think. The next thing is premises." He paused and let out a cry. "Why, I've got the very thing. Mr Williams has a small basement in St Peter's Street off Wardour Street he was using as a cellar. It wasn't big enough to hold his stock of best plonk reserved for the West End, and he's just taken over the lease of a larger place in Berwick Street. Hang on, and I'll give him a call right now."

Five minutes later Tibbs came back laughing. "We're on Captain."

"You're a genius, Tibbs," I said.

For the remainder of the evening we discussed details of the scheme. Shortly before we parted Tibbs frowned and said. "Do you know we've forgotten one thing, Captain?"

"What's that?"

"The cunt."

"That's where you're wrong," I said. "Nothing could be easier. Haven't you noticed how few girls there are on the streets because of the freeze-up? They're having to operate from the pubs and the classier ones from hotel foyers. I bet you I can find a thousand who will be willing to take off their clothes in the warmth of our basement. What's more they won't have to be mauled about by a lot of strangers. To put it crudely, they won't have to toss off a lot of old men, let alone be fucked by them."

We arranged to meet at the basement in St Peter's the next day at midday, shook hands, and departed in high spirits, dreaming of yachts in the Mediterranean, and the millions of pounds that were ours for the picking.

I arrived back at Mavis's flat soon after midnight. When she asked me where I had been, I decided to keep quiet about the project until I had got it off the ground. So I told her I had been out with an old friend, which was true in its way.

Before meeting Tibbs the next morning I made my way to the block of flats in Jermyn Street now exclusively occupied by tarts, where I had stayed before being ejected by the landlord. While I had been there I had become quite friendly with one of the girls.

Jean was not exactly pleased to see me. "Christ, Mike, can't you let a girl have a lie in after she's been working all night?"

"Have you been working?" I said. "I understand that this blizzard has somewhat damped the ardour of your clients."

Jean nodded ruefully. "It's too bloody cold to work outside, too bloody right. Anyway, what brings you here? Don't tell me that you've suddenly taken a fancy to me."

"I've always fancied you."

"I suppose it's something really kinky you're after."

"No, no Jean. Just listen to this and tell me what you think."

I told her the outlines of the scheme that Tibbs and I had hatched the previous night.

Jean listened carefully. When I had finished she said: "I can't fault it, Mike. As far as I'm concerned you can count me in. What about the cash?"

"Ten per cent of the gross."

"What the bloody hell does that mean in English?"

"It means ten per cent of every piece of money we take from every source. Entrance money, soft drinks masquerading as Napoleon brandy, the lot. In other words for every hundred quid we take you collect ten."

"It doesn't sound much," said Jean.

"It's a new venture. If it goes you'll make hundreds a week." I pointed at the window. "It's cold outside in the street, isn't it Jean?"

"You bastard," she said. She paused. "Sure you don't want a fuck right now? I'll give you a good time."

"Business calls" I said, although I was tempted. "Come on over to St Peter's Street about six this evening, and we'll show you the set up." I wrote down the number on a piece of paper and hurried off to meet Tibbs.

Tibbs and Jean took to one another immediately, and the three of us set about getting the basement into some kind of shape. Together we whitewashed the walls and at one end we erected a somewhat shaky stage on which Jean would perform. Tibbs had come across half a dozen electric lanterns in Berwick Market, and we hung them from the walls to provide what we thought a mysterious and sexy light. We decided against any initial expenditure on chairs. I had to confess that the end product was somewhat stark, more like a convict's cell on Dartmoor than the interior of a smart night club. The problem of heating was overcome by the purchase of three ancient Valour stoves, again from Berwick Market, where Tibbs seemed to wield considerable influence. They smelt abominably, but as Tibbs remarked "The customers will be so hooked on cunt, they won't notice fuck-all else."

As to how Jean should perform and what we should do, Tibbs and I gave her a free hand. "You've just got to bring the poor sods on so that they come back for more punishment," said Tibbs. We had in fact nothing to worry about. In her younger days Jean had danced in the chorus, and had only given up her career when she decided that the oldest profession in the world was a surer way to riches.

Once again Tibbs was dispatched to Berwick Market, and returned staggering under the weight of an ancient H.M.V. gramophone. "Got some good records too. Charlie Kunz at the old joanna. Charlie Kunz, quite appropriate, don't you think?"

For the dress rehearsal, with only myself and Tibbs as the audience, Jean had dolled herself in a pair of beach trousers with a tight waisted jacket on top.

As soon as the music started she stepped up on the stage and started to wiggle about. First she removed the jacket, and then the trousers. She was a genius, for she was wearing a two-piece swim suit. I need go no further into the details of that great strip, except to say that she ended up with absolutely nothing on, undulating to the music as she showed us everything with which nature had endowed her.

"Christ," muttered Tibbs. "That hasn't half brought me on. What about you, Captain?"

"Me too."

"We can't fail, ducks," he shouted out. "The Captain's got a right hard on, and if you can do it to the old bugger, you'll make the youngsters knock the roof off."

"That's a bit unkind, Tibbs," I said. "I'll have you know I'm only twenty-five."

"But you've given it a lot of wear and tear in its time, Captain," said Tibbs.

We were all excited and confident that nothing could go wrong.

After a few drinks at the Intrepid Fox round the corner, we decided that there was no point in waiting; that we would open the following night. Tibbs undertook to collect the entrance money at the door which we set at a modest five shillings, while Jean and I would run the bar until the time came for her to perform. Tibbs agreed to pay a further visit to Berwick Market in the morning and rake up a few glasses and mugs for the lemonade with which to slake the customers' thirst who, we reckoned, would be gasping after watching Jean's performance.

We decided that only a few guests should be invited to the opening night. We wanted to keep the riff-raff out. Tibbs was sure that his boss Mr Williams would be interested and would bring along a small but select party. I knew George Holmes would do the same, and Jean said she had a member of the House of Lords among her clientele, who had long ago exhausted everything in the book. She reckoned if her show brought him on, we would be millionaires for certain.

The opening night was a resounding success. There were about twenty guests present. Jean performed three times, dancing for about ten minutes on each occasion. I made a note to buy a second gramophone, as it continually needed rewinding which marred the continuity of her choreography. I must say she was marvellous and threw her whole body and soul into the spirit of the game, becoming sexier and sexier as the evening went on. At the end she had so successfully stimulated her member of the Upper House that he whisked her off to the Ritz to spend the night with him, and no doubt give him relief from nervous tension.

Ever since I went into the strip business I am convinced that, if you have a good product, there is no need to spend money on advertising. After three nights we were jammed to the doors, and turning customers away. I was slightly annoyed with George when he turned up on the second night in the company of a couple of detectives, but he assured me afterwards that they had enjoyed the show so much that they would tell their friends and we had no fear of prosecution. It was George who pointed out that from the publicity point of view we should give the club a name so that it would be easily identifiable to new members.

"That's bloody simple," said Tibbs. "Let's call it the Captain's Cabin."

I am still proud that London's first strip club should have been named after me.

In spite of the blizzard that continued to rage outside, by the end of the week we were turning customers away, and had taken just short of one hundred and fifty pounds in cash, which must be the equivalent of nearly a thousand pounds today. This, of course, included the proceeds from soft drinks. We decided not to attempt to sell alcohol in the club for fear of running up against the law and because in my experience nearly all aggravation is brought on by booze. We also decided not to open on Sundays in case the Lord's Day Observance Society should hear of our activities and start to complain that we were profaning the Sabbath. Tibbs on the other hand rightly pointed out that we were not exploiting the potential of the Captain's Cabin to the full.

"It's like a racecourse. Only used a few days a year and lying idle the rest."

"What do you mean?"

"It's daft only to open in the evenings. We could pack the cabin all day long. There's thousands and thousands of horny blokes roaming round London with their pockets stuffed with cash, only too ready to give it away for the sight of a bit of tit."

"Tibbs is right," said Jean. "But I don't think I could do more than the evening show, otherwise my art might suffer."

I saw Tibbs was about to make some pertinent remark about Jean's art so I hurriedly said: "You're absolutely right, Jean darling. There is a limit to what the true artiste like yourself can do. I suggest you look around among your fellow artistes and see if you can find anybody who would stand in for you."

Tibbs did not take kindly to the artistic quality that Jean wanted to bring to the show. Later on he said to me when Jean was not present: "Let's forget all this artistic crap, Captain. You know perfectly well all that the silly sods want to see is a bint with no clothes on so that they can go off and have a quiet wank. By the way what are we going to do about the poor buggers that toss themselves off under their macs?"

"What can we do?" I said.

"What about putting up a notice 'No Wanking Here'?" suggested Tibbs.

We had opened on the Monday and I spent the Sunday quietly with Mavis at her room in Lupus Street. Up to then I had told her very little of my scheme, but I was so assured of its success that I now let her into my secret and explained why I had been coming home so late at night.

"Sounds all right to me, Mick," she commented. "At least the poor girls don't have to walk the streets in this awful weather. I suppose you could say too that you're offering a kind of service to the blokes. Did you really make all that money? One hundred and fifty quid in a week?"

"That's right. And the end of next week you can choose yourself something fancy. What would you like? What about some flash jewellery?"

"No thanks, Mick. If you really mean it, what I need is a warm coat. I nearly freeze to death every day between here and work."

"You're on," I said. I put my arms round her and gave her a hug.

"I'm so glad for you, Mick," she said. "I hope your luck holds for you."

On Monday afternoon Tibbs and I were getting the club tidied up for the evening performance when Jean arrived with a blonde girl whom she introduced to us as Norma.

When we had shaken hands I said: "Can you dance, Norma?"

Norma looked taken aback. "What do you think? Here, do you want to see my cuttings?"

From her bag she took out half a dozen dog-eared photographs of chorus girls in a line.

"There, that's me at the far end. I'm afraid he was a very poor photographer who took this, not up to the standard of the ones I usually engage."

"Has Jean explained what we want you to do here? I mean to put it crudely: have you any objection to removing your clothes in front of a lot of blokes?"

"Why the hell should I? I'm not ashamed of my body am I? Only too pleased if it gives them a thrill."

"Perhaps you would like to give us a demonstration," I said. I turned to Tibbs. "Music, maestro, please."

Tibbs wound up the gramophone, and put on a record. Norma, having taken off her overcoat, climbed onto the stage and started to perform.

I could see at once that she was not a patch on Jean. She bumped and ground round the small stage putting everything that she had got into the performance, but all she succeeded in doing was looking ludicrous.

"How's that?" she asked panting heavily when the music stopped.

"Very nice, dear," I said having learned my lesson from watching the great C. B. Cochran that an impresario must always be polite at auditions.

Tibbs who had not had the privilege of watching the great man at work said: "Bloody awful."

Norma flared up. "What did you say?"

"Shut up, Tibbs," I said.

"She'll drive them out into the street or turn them all queer," Tibbs muttered under his breath.

I think Jean was delighted at Tibbs's criticism of the performance we had just witnessed. It confirmed her belief in herself that she was a true artiste, which indeed she was. Since that day I have seen hundreds of strippers go through their paces. There are those who can project sex-appeal and there are those who cannot. The most beautiful girl can remove her clothes and leave an audience cold, while a moderately good-looking girl can keep her clothes on and have her audience sitting on the edges of their seats drooling with lust.

Jean climbed onto the stage. "Here, just you watch, Norma, and try to follow me," she said. "Music, maestro, and could you find something a bit slower. Got a waltz or something like that?"

"How about the Blue Danube?" said Tibbs. "The Blue Danube for a blue show."

As Jean went into her impromptu routine I found myself watching her with growing appreciation. When the record came to its end and the needle was scratching in the groove, I was still staring at her and wanting more. For the first time since my disaster with Julia in Paris, I found myself excited.

Jean must have sensed what was going through my mind, for she came and stood next to me. She was warm from her dancing, and I could smell her perspiration mixed with scent emanating from her body.

"You liked that didn't you, you naughty boy?" she said.

I was sitting down and she moved close to me so that her dressing gown which she had put across her shoulders after she had finished dancing swung open to reveal her nakedness.

My lascivious thoughts were interrupted by Tibbs.

"Captain, I've got the most bloody wonderful idea. An absolute winner. Two bloody girls. That's the answer."

"What do you mean?" I said.

Jean understood what Tibbs was getting at straight away. "He's right. Two girls, three girls, as many girls as you like. You could even bring on a fellow or two. The possibilities are endless, absolutely endless."

I could see that she was really excited. "Perhaps you would explain?"

"Don't you see?" she said. "We can go in for the kinky stuff. Lots of my clients like to see me making love to another girl. I've got one old fellow who has long passed it, who likes to watch me being fucked by a young man."

"Steady on," I said. "The Captain's Cabin is a respectable club, and I intend to keep it that way."

"You're probably right, Mike," said Jean. "But we should bear it in mind for the future."

We opened our doors at seven that evening and put on our first show at eight. I had been right about Norma. She failed to have any impact on the audience, and I was relieved when she was followed by Jean who had the desired effect and brought the company to the necessary peak of enjoyment.

I was having a drink with one of the customers when someone touched me on the arm. It was Jean. She looked nervous.

I excused myself and followed her across the packed room to the door.

Two men, both dark and small, were waiting for me.

"Good-evening," I said. "I trust that you are enjoying the show?"

They looked at me, and I had a nasty feeling that they were weighing me up.

"You the Captain?" asked one.

"I suppose you could say that."

"You own this joint?"

"In partnership."

"We don't like it," he said. He turned to his companion. "We don't like it, Tony, do we?"

"It's disgusting," said Tony. "No respectable girl should be seen taking off her clothes in front of a crowd of fellows."

I thought I detected a foreign accent in both their voices. It was dark in the club, but it seemed to me that my two visitors were of Italian extraction.

"I'm sorry you don't like the show," I said. "In which case you can have your money back." I took out a ten shilling note and held it towards them.

The man who had first addressed me ignored it and said: "I have never seen such filth in my life. You may finish your exhibition tonight. But that is the end. Tomorrow you will be off the manor."

"Who the hell do you think you are?" I said.

"It doesn't matter who we are. We will not have such filth on our manor."

Before I could say any more they turned and walked out of the club.

"What does that mean, Jean? Who are they?"

Jean looked frightened. "I don't like it. Not one little bit."

"They're just a couple of bloody wops trying to throw their weight about," I said.

When the show finished that night, our main topic of conversation was the visit of the two strangers. Jean was clearly scared, but undertook to make enquiries the following day to see what she could find out about them.

Tibbs and I, although worried, agreed that on no account would we close down unless we were confronted by a superior force.

We opened the following night as usual. Jean was still worried, although she had not been able to discover anything about the two strangers who had visited the club the previous evening. The Captain's Cabin was packed. The audience was appreciative and even Norma received a reasonable ovation and I was pleased to see how quickly she was learning from watching Jean.

At the end of the evening when we counted our takings we were delighted to find that they came to the record sum of fifty pounds.

"If we go on this way I shall be able to marry, settle down in the country and bring up a family," said Jean.

"Are you being serious?"

"What do you think I went on the game for? As soon as I've got enough cash together you won't see my backside for dust."

We went round to the Intrepid Fox, had a few drinks, and continued to discuss the future. By closing time, Tibbs and I had persuaded Jean that she should stay with us and make a million. As Tibbs put it: "You've got it all wrong about your arse. They'll pay to see your backside with gold dust."

The following day I met Tibbs at the Intrepid Fox at about six o'clock. We were still both excited at the profitable way our enterprise was going and we discussed ways and means of improving it. We were agreed on one thing. Soon we should have to move into larger and less sordid surroundings. Tibbs was for taking over the London Palladium but I was in favour of keeping the club small and intimate. I pointed out that if necessary we would open a chain of small clubs in London and that there was nothing to prevent us taking a look at the provinces.

About half past six we wandered round the corner to the club.

As soon as we reached the bottom of the basement steps I knew that something was wrong. In the dim light cast by the street lamp above I saw that the door was open.

I pushed my hand against it and it fell backwards.

"What the hell's going on?" I said.

I went into the club and put down the switch inside the door. To my surprise only one light came on. But it was enough.

"Fuck me," said Tibbs.

The Captain's Cabin was a shambles. Whoever had done it had made a thorough job of it. Stage, chairs, bars, gramophone, curtains, all the lamps save the one that cast its light on the scene of complete destruction had been smashed and torn to smithereens. The floors and walls had been covered with oil and soot.

"Someone doesn't like us," said Tibbs.

He walked past me into the club.

"The filthy bastards" he said.

On the floor someone had urinated and defecated.

I felt sick. "Let's get out of here," I said, "before I bring up."

We were both considerably shaken and hurried back to the Intrepid Fox.

"What do we do now?" I said.

"The first thing is to find Jean and see if she's all right," said Tibbs. "You realize that she should have been here at six."

We were lucky enough to find a taxi in spite of the fact that it was still snowing outside. We paid it off in Jermyn Street.

There was no answer when we knocked on Jean's door, but I could see there was a light coming under the door.

"Jean, it's me and Tibbs," I called.

The door was opened and Tibbs and I went in.

Jean had a couple of suitcases on the bed and was in the middle of packing.

"The club's been wrecked."

"I know," she said.

"What goes on?" I asked.

"Please, Mike, don't ask me too much."

I could see that she was scared out of her wits.

"Was it those two men?"

She nodded. "Please, Mike, go away and leave me alone."

"Have they been threatening you?"

"Yes." She put out a finger and drew it down the side of her face.

"The bastards," said Tibbs. "Who are they Jean?"

She hesitated. "If I tell you, will you promise never to mention it to another soul?"

I nodded.

"I don't know much about them," said Jean, "but I've made a few enquiries and quite a lot of the girls have heard of them. They're known as the Sicilian Mob. There's all kinds of rumours about them, and everyone says they're connected with the Mafia."

I did not like the sound of that one bit. Remembering how I had double-crossed the Mafia in Naples, I wasn't keen to mix with their brothers from Sicily.

"What's their racket?" said Tibbs.

"Rumour has it that they're going to take over all the prostitution in the West End. They reckon that the days of the amateur girls are coming to an end as the Yanks and the rest go home, and they want to control all the professionals. It's said they're recruiting a heavy mob to bring us into line."

"Why did they break up our club? We're not even in the prostitution business," said Tibbs.

"I don't know. One of the girls I spoke to says they really do think it's disgusting."

"Come off it," I said.

"It's true. They're very family minded and the idea of a girl stripping doesn't seem right to them. On the other hand they may think you're creaming off some of the trade. Whatever the reason they don't like you."

"You can say that again," said Tibbs.

"And now will you go, please," said Jean. "I must finish my packing."

"Where are you going?" I asked.

"Please don't ask any more questions," said Jean. "Please, please go."

"All right," I said. "Here, if you want to get in touch with me, you can write to me here." I tore out a page from my diary, wrote down the address of Coutts & Co. and handed it to her.

"Poor kid," said Tibbs. "They must have scared the daylights out of you."

"If they cut me up I don't stand a chance at my game," said Jean.

"Isn't there anything we can do?" I said. "I mean do we have to put up with this kind of thing?" I turned to Tibbs. "For Christ's sake, Tibbs, this is England, not bloody Italy. If they'd tried anything on like that while we were there we would have beaten the daylights out of the buggers."

"It's not the same any longer, Captain," said Tibbs. "This is dear old England 1947. Things have changed."

"Please, please go," said Jean.

"All right, love," I said. I put my arms round her, and kissed her. "See you soon," I said. "I hope one day you'll find that nice young man, that place in the country and have lots and lots of babies."

I think she was too frightened to hear what I said.

There is little more I can write about the Captain's Cabin, except to say that it never opened again.

Tibbs and I discussed the situation from every conceivable angle. We made enquiries through George Holmes's friends in the police, who confirmed what Jean had told us. What is more they predicted an outbreak of gang warfare in London's West End as the Sicilian Mob started to move in, and this proved to be the case.

We were both extremely bitter to have to admit defeat especially at the hands of a load of wops whom we had so despised both in Africa and in their own country. But we both agreed that having survived the war, it was stupid to end up in a gutter in Soho with a cut throat. Applying the principles of war, we reluctantly concluded that the only answer to an untenable position was a hasty retreat.

Nevertheless even today I am bitter at the failure of the Captain's Cabin. My idea was several years in advance of its time. That, of course, is the misfortune that befalls every genius.

Round about 1968 Jilly Cooper asked me to accompany her on a round of the Soho Strip Clubs about which she was writing an article for *The Sunday Times*. They had advanced a great deal from the days of the Captain's Cabin, but the basic principle was the same. I was amused too to see that Tibbs had been right. The permutations that Jilly and I saw on the stages were innumerable. Two girls performing was basic stuff. In one establishment we saw eight girls and a python.

# Epilogue

The arctic conditions grew worse. The railways froze up, the little coal that came out of the pits, whose equipment had become obsolete during the years of war, failed to reach the factories, let alone the homes of the unfortunate people. Unemployment rose to over two million. A great malaise descended upon the British Isles. The nation was clapped out, tired, frozen and bolshie. It was becoming clear to everyone that we may have won the war but we had lost the peace.

After the wrecking of the Captain's Cabin I lay for two days in Mavis's bed licking my wounds, and considering my future. The more I considered it the blacker it grew. I had no qualifications. I was just one of millions of men and women discharged from the forces with no ability or skill.

On the third day Mavis became angry. "You can't lie there for the rest of your life. You might as well go along to the Labour Exchange and see if there's anything going."

"Well, they might want someone to sweep the snow off the streets," I said.

"That's better than nothing," she said.

I took her advice and later that morning after she had gone to work I walked through the blizzard to the Labour Exchange and joined a long queue to sign on.

The clerk who finally interviewed me seemed to think I was a bit of surplus equipment. After I had told him of my years of dedication and service to my country in foreign parts he remarked: "That's all very well, Mr Nelson, but about the only thing you can do is drive a lorry, and I've got hundreds of people like you on the books."

"So no one wants me?"

"Not at the moment, Mr Nelson."

I left the Labour Exchange in a greater state of dejection than when I had entered it. Going down Victoria Street my mood was not improved when I passed a street band of old soldiers shuffling along in the ice-bound gutter. On an impulse I turned round and went up to the man rattling the collection box.

"Any future in this game?" I enquired.

He shook his head. "Bloody rough in this weather. No, mate, fuck all in it."

I decided then and there against a street musicians' band.

When I got back to Mavis's room I had come to the conclusion that London was not the place for me; that I had no intention of hanging around its bars and hostelries sponging on friends and acquaintances now that my cash was running short. But the question was, what was I to do?

I sat down at the table in Mavis's room and took up a pencil and placed a sheet of paper in front of me. What could I do? What had I learnt if anything during the last five years in the army?

With my pencil I wrote: TIME SPENT IN RECONNAISSANCE IS SELDOM WASTED. That was perfectly true. I had reconnoitered the streets of London and had found that they contained no gold for me.

I paused for a minute and then I wrote: II MAI. In other words, the eleventh of May in French. I should explain that these symbols stand for INFORMATION, INTENTION, METHOD, ADMINISTRATION, INTERCOMMUNICATION. This was the way the army taught its soldiers to issue orders. Montgomery used this system when sending men over the top at the battle of Alamein, just as I used it in sending mine to disaster in the battle of Anzio, where I committed the error of giving an incorrect map reference so that six of my merry men were taken prisoners.

I then proceeded to fill up the piece of paper as follows:
INFORMATION. Situation desperate. No work. Bank balance low but you do have £5 a week coming in.
INTENTION. To survive. How? The only thing you can do is to write. So write a best seller.
METHOD. Find somewhere to live cheaply in the country. Cut out all booze.
ADMINISTRATION. Set about questioning friends and enemies for possible country retreat.
INTERCOMMUNICATION. There will be none. You will not come near London until you have completed your masterpiece.

Looking back I think now that my intention to become a writer was the wrong one. So far I have never written a best seller. Nor have I ever come to enjoy writing. But I suppose that is another story, although I would strongly advise all girls and boys against writing for a living. But at the time it seemed my only asset, after my failures to acclimatize myself to the ways of Civvy Street. My intention was also probably helped by a growing dislike for the sheer sleaziness of London. At least in the country I would breathe fresh air. Before I had come home London had seemed Mecca to me, but six months as a civilian had turned me from a happy warrior returning home, to a disillusioned wreck.

Two weeks later, about the middle of April, I heard of a ruin in Essex which I was able to rent without viewing for three pounds a week. As soon as I saw it I nearly asked the taxi driver to turn about and take me back to the station. The place had been almost burned to the ground, the pillars of the portico were collapsing beneath the weight of the ice and snow. The wind howled across what had once been the park, but which had long ago been denuded of trees.

"You're not going to live there, are you?" said the driver.

I think it was this remark that made me decide to stay. I felt that after all my recent disasters and failures I could not face another one. I could not run for ever.

After the taxi had turned and gone, I dug my way, using my hands, through the snow to the side door. I then humped all my worldly possession into a room that had been roughly converted into a kitchen. I managed to get some kind of fire under way and made myself a cup of tea. But I had first, like Scott in the Antarctic, to melt snow to obtain the water.

The taps were frozen solid and so was the lavatory. Remembering all that I had been taught about hygiene by the army, I decided that the first thing to do was to erect a temporary latrine. I unrolled my valise and took out my old battle dress and put it on top of my demob suit, and went out into the blizzard. With the aid of a piece of wood I scooped a hole in the snow. The tea must have activated my bowels, because I was suddenly overcome with the urge to crap. I pulled down both pairs of trousers and crouched down as the wind howled round me, and the snow beat against my buttocks.

I happened to look down and saw my campaign medals, stained and grimey on the front of my battle dress.

That it should come to this, I thought to myself. But I am glad to say that not for a moment did I feel sorry for myself. I did think of blue Italian skies, of my batmen Lane and Tibbs, of my friend John Fish, of my adorable Lucia, as I squatted there in the snow. But they had been the exceptions to the horror and the boredom of those war years.

Captain Blossom was back in Civvy Street. Captain Blossom now knew where he was going. He had recovered his determination to succeed.

It's just as well that Captain Blossom did not know as he squatted in the snow that his first novel, which was to go by the appalling title of *The Coming of the Void*, would be read by fifty-five publishers, and rejected by every single one.